Praise

"A spectacular read! How inspiring to see how the women highlighted in *Your True Power* have faced their fears and overcome the obstacles from past trauma to rise like phoenixes from the fire and create better lives. I felt my heart open more and more with each story."

Marci Shimoff | #1 *New York Times* bestselling author of *Happy for No Reason* and *Chicken Soup for the Woman's Soul*

"*Your True Power* is a life-changer! Each author took me on a deep transformational journey through the most challenging times of their lives to emerge from their experience not broken and bitter, but victorious as they are now happier, healthier, and even more loved and fulfilled than ever! On top of that, each author gives their unique 'how to' create this kind of massive transformation in an easy and implementable way in one's own life! *Your True Power* is a personal development masterpiece! I recommend this book to all that are ready to embrace and finally live the bigger and greater life that they know is waiting for them!"

Rikka Zimmerman| Founder and Creator of Life Transformed

"In this day and age, perhaps the iconic clash between David and Goliath would be more accurately represented as one person, not fighting against a figurative giant, but against their own mind and limiting self-beliefs. This was exactly the sentiment I got in reading *Your True Power*. Each vignette was a powerful battle of one woman trying to take back all that she had unknowingly given away, and in so doing, coming closer and closer to her most authentic self."

Dr. Bradley Nelson | author of *The Emotion Code* and creator of *The Body Code*

"Never has there been a more important time for women to step into their authentic power! This delightful collection of stories of 14 ordinary women who did exactly that will inspire and motivate you to step up and step into your magnificence."

Petrea King | Founder and CEO, Quest for Life Centre; author of *Your Life Matters*

"*Your True Power* contains the full spectrum of human emotions and I felt them all. You simply can't help but be drawn into each beautiful story. If my heart hurt in hearing about the emotional, psychological and physical abuse some of these women endured, it did somersaults in watching them triumph over their circumstances with grace and maturity. A must read for men and women!"

Mark Anthony Lord | spiritual teacher, healer, and author

Every once in a while you read something that just hits differently, something you know you'll never be able to forget – *Your True Power* is exactly that. From the very first chapter I didn't want to put it down. Each of the narratives is so different and yet so powerfully relevant at the same time. More than just the stories themselves, it was the profound honesty of each of the women throughout the book that truly moved me.

Mary Morrissey | Best-Selling Author and Founder, Brave Thinking Institute

"Emotional. Poignant. Inspiring. *Your True Power* was a roller coaster of a read that beautifully chronicles the lives of women from all over the world reaffirming their own value and self-worth. After finishing the book I felt as if I had lived several lifetimes. I would highly recommend this to anyone who feels they have lost their way, or given up something precious of themselves."

Steve Olsher | Founder & Editor-in-Chief, Podcast Magazine; *New York Times* bestselling author of *What Is Your WHAT?*

"*Your True Power* is a counter-narrative to a society that often goads women into questioning their value. Through each iterative chapter of the book, we see women transcend dire circumstances in their marriages, family life, and careers, as well as the pressures of societal expectations, through the realization and recognition of their innate Spiritual power, strength, and resiliency. Let their testimonials inspire you to discover your greatness and create a life of beauty, wonder, and joy."

Michael Bernard Beckwith | Founder & Spiritual Director, Agape International Spiritual Center; Author, Life Visioning and Spiritual Liberation

Contents

Introduction

What would it be like for you to have true power?

For thousands of years, legends and tales have characterized *power* to be in the realm of the deity, magic, witchcraft, sorcery, wizards, dragons, kings, and nobility. Nowadays, these tales have become embodied by genies, fairy godmothers, superheroes, and mutants.

Do you know that the top five highest-grossing movies of all time have elements of magic and fantasy? We rush to theatres or binge-watch these stories from our couches to experience our heroes saving the day—because, deep down, we all wish we were that powerful. In reality, we feel helpless. We desire so desperately to change the way people see us, to find a way to control our success. We think if only we were prettier, faster, richer, or smarter, then somehow, life would be easier.

If you were like me and most other kids, you too imagined having superpowers as a child. You may have watched superheroes on TV and wished you had the same capabilities. The heroes didn't seem to have to work hard. They were lucky and just had these special gifts that made them important. They made a difference, and people just loved them. Of course, who wouldn't want to have superpowers!

You may not remember, but you were born with the power to get everything you needed and wanted.

You came out crying, smiling, and giggling, and you easily got attention, love, and nourishment. But one day, it seemed like none of that was enough. You needed to work harder and to do or not do certain things for Mom and Dad to give you love and affection: use your spoon and fork, don't make a mess, finish your food, then you can play. If not, you were yelled at or punished. You lost your power.

Your young mind couldn't really make sense of what was happening, but you had to do whatever it took to survive and be loved.

So you—and virtually everyone else—have grown up looking for this power that you once had, mostly without knowing it.

We transitioned through life and found ourselves stuck in either difficult relationships, financial stress, physical pain, chronic anxiety, or some form of suffering and addiction. A major crisis came—a global pandemic, the sudden death of a loved one, loss of income, divorce, terminal illness, accidents… Things fell apart, and we felt powerless.

We learned in school and from peers, family, movies, advertisements, and our very own experiences that it is money, position, sex, beauty, physical strength, talent, intelligence, material wealth, and fame that dictate who has power. It's the President, the professional star athlete, the social media influencer, the rock star, the Hollywood celebrity, the reality show star made famous by her sex scandal, and the guys smart enough to invent a game-changing software that hold the power and enjoy the good life.

At the same time, it's not uncommon to hear about the same very successful people suffering, sometimes to the point of suicide. Hollywood actor Robin Williams, fashion designer Kate Spade, celebrity chef and journalist Anthony Bourdain, and billionaire Adolf Merckle are examples of very successful people who ended their life despite appearing to have it all. Many of those who look great from the outside eye are often suffering deeply inside. This teaches us that external accomplishment is a dangling carrot that doesn't bring true success.

Most people cruise through life and accept that struggling and pain are part of it. I'm here to tell you that they don't have to be.

When you live in your true power, blissful relationships, a vibrantly healthy body, and financial abundance are the new normal. Life is filled with love, ease, joy, flow, and freedom. Magic, miracles, and healing are in your everyday life. You feel loved, supported, worthy, and powerful.

Through this anthology, you will be inspired by fourteen true stories of ordinary women who overcame, and recovered from, their biggest, darkest challenges—such as heartbreaks, betrayals, failures, burnouts, chronic stress and illness, abuse, imprisonment, and depression—when they realized their true power.

They unleashed this capacity by walking through despair all the way to an amazing life beyond their imaginations. By reading their experiences, you will gain an understanding of what true power is. With different stories, points of view, and voices illustrating one and the same message, you will gain a well-rounded sense of what true power is. You will learn that *Your True Power* is the key to your amazing life.

Since I was a young girl, I was obsessed with true success. I wanted to enjoy real happiness in every area of my life—to be, do, and have anything I wanted, when I wanted it. This put me on the path to becoming a transformational executive coach and interviewing the world's top thought leaders and successful entrepreneurs. Studying books, taking courses, hiring mentors, and deploying immense willpower have helped me take big leaps. But no matter how much I added on to my skills, optimized my strategies, or enhanced my mindset, something else was missing. Part of me was still suffering. After more than twenty years, over a hundred thousand dollars, and loads of tears later, I found the last piece of the puzzle.

I found my true power.

From this space, there is no need to accomplish, no pressure to do anything, no demand to get anywhere. It's all play, joy, and bliss. So I asked Source to show me what's next for me. I wondered what would be the most fun thing to do.

The guidance that came so strongly to me is to get together with my soul family (women with whom I have shared deep transformation work), together magnifying our true power and channeling it as co-authors through this book and out to the world!

With a big resounding *yes* in their hearts, fourteen co-authors have come together to be the unstoppable force of true power. I've personally witnessed these remarkable women terribly lost in the depths of suffering come through to the other side. They have found the key. They have the answer. They will show you the way out.

It is no coincidence that this book is being birthed in the midst of the global pandemic. It is divine timing.

The world needs to know this message now more than ever. In times of crisis, it is not the time to shrink— rather it is the time to rise up! The planet needs to wake up to the truth that there is no circumstance greater or more powerful than your true power.

None of the coauthors are professional writers, they are ordinary women simply sharing their personal stories from the heart. We are one heart with one intention of bringing the entire planet in true power.

Imagine yourself completely happy, abundant, and free.

Now imagine 7.8 billion people absolutely happy, abundant, and free. What would this world be like?

Zero suffering and only pure bliss for everything and everyone!

The sole mission of this anthology is to inspire you to live in your true power. If you think any of this is a fairytale, over the top, or impossible, then these fourteen women are here to testify that magic is real. We aim to take you through the journey of our rock-bottom moments and peak transformations, so you can feel and know what's truly possible for you. If we can do it, so can you.

This is not a how-to book. It is not meant to provide you step-by-step instructions, but rather to inspire you to make a choice and take the leap into the amazing life that is already waiting for you.

To take care of the how-to and to provide you with the next steps, we do have a free companion resource to this book, the *Your True Power Toolkit*. It is a collection of the best tools the coauthors recommend to get you immediately started in accessing your true power. Every coauthor has shared a tool corresponding to their chapter that served them best. They are meant to be bite-size, easily implementable steps that you can use to experience transformation right away. You can download the toolkit for free at www.yourtruepowerbook.com or https:// bit.ly/yourtruepowerbook.

The chapters are arranged in three sections: Discovering Your True Power, Stepping into Your True Power, and Living in Your True Power. At the back of this book, you will find photos and bios of each of the authors so that you can learn more about them. If you resonate with any of the stories and coauthors, I highly encourage you to reach out and connect with them.

All fourteen authors are so deeply committed to this movement of *Your True Power* that book sales proceeds will go back to spreading our core message and to charity.

It is no accident that you are reading this book. You have over seven hundred years of combined life experience within your grasp. You are ready for more. You are ready to live in heaven on earth. Your amazing life is here now!

Trissa Tismal-Capili
July 2020

PART 1

DISCOVERING YOUR TRUE POWER

A Quest for True Success

Trissa Tismal-Capili

I moved to Los Angeles a few months ago. I just left a successful continuing legal education company I cofounded in the Philippines. After innovating the industry to make it fun and not just another required drudgery, working with top lawyers, judges, and Supreme Court Justices, I was burned out. I realized I was working hard for something I didn't like.

So here I embark on a quest to find what I'd love to do throughout my life! I left my relatively spoiled life at home and bade goodbye to the comforts of maids, family, and friends for this big adventure! To not burden my parents, I'm making sure I neither ask for money nor help. I'm in my early twenties, bold, and fearless. I don't care how hard it gets. I will figure it all out!

For months, I've been asking every successful person I meet how they made their fortune, got into their business, and found their passion. Among them is AJ, CEO and publisher of *Long Beach Magazine*, who tells me, "Trissa, I think you'd be an excellent life coach!"

"Really? What's a life coach? I've never heard of that."

"It's what you're already doing right now. You're a great listener, you're very positive and motivational, you have a knack for helping people, and most of all, you think big." He continues saying all the reasons why it's a good fit for me.

My eyes light up. "Wow, that sounds really great!"

I rush back home. Right now, home is a motel room just a few steps away from Seal Beach. I google *life coach* to learn more. Not much is written about it yet. The coaching profession is brand-new. The world doesn't know about it, and from what I'm reading, it's a career and business made for me!

"Ah! Yes, yes!" I'm so happy. I'm dancing, jumping, shouting for joy! In just a short time, I've found what I was looking for! All the positive-thinking and self-growth books I've been reading since sixth grade do work!

I'm bright-eyed and excited to transform and save the world. "Get ready, world. I'm coming to soak you in positivity! I'm going to have it all and live the dream!"

Just like in anything I do, I go all in. I attend a life coaching school while waiting tables and working at a financial advisor firm in downtown LA.

Halfway through coaching school, I start getting clients by sharing with everyone I'm a life coach. I do so with bursting enthusiasm, which everyone must have felt. My sample sessions amazed them, and they became my first clients. It was that easy. It also happens that these clients are successful multimillion-dollar businessmen.

I'm having so much fun, fulfillment, and satisfaction in witnessing my clients' success. It feels like I'm living in a dream.

But I'm only getting started. I'm not stopping until I become like my heroes—Tony Robbins, Robin Sharma, Zig Ziglar, Dale Carnegie.... The transformation they made in the world is indelible and profoundly awe-inspiring. I've always had this drive to be, do, and have everything. Despite coming from a third-world country, witnessing intense poverty, corruption, and suffering, deep in my heart, I believe it's possible.

I'm carefully studying and following the teachings of the most prominent success leaders:

Seeking perfection matters.
Always improve and innovate daily.
Outwork, outlearn, outdo everyone in your industry.
Being complacent will lead to your downfall.
Overdeliver to your clients.
Sacrifice now and reap the rewards later.
Ignore criticisms.
Follow what the masters have done.
Suck up the challenges and hardships; it's meant to be really hard.
Work very, very hard.

Each day, I practice what I preach—joining masterminds, hiring coaches, getting more professional training and certifications. I make sure I learn from the leading industry experts and implement all I've learned in my work. All this requires tons of focus and willpower, and without knowing it, I am burning out more than ever.

I'm continually changing myself and too willing to do whatever it takes. Deep down, I'm a happy, giggly, bouncy, perky person, unfit to be a traditional coach. What I truly am is not how the so-called professionals are, so I must force myself to fit inside the box and practice suppressing my natural joy to look more professional and mature.

My gift for positivity is instrumental in putting my problems aside—the deportation threats, the constant criticisms from my brother, or the toxic marriage I've gotten myself into. It doesn't matter if I'm under chronic stress, repeatedly getting sick from lack of sleep, because they're just setbacks I needed to overcome. I go out with a big smile, convincing myself and the world I got this—nothing to worry about!

Then comes the mountains of emails—the to-dos, the constant grind of generating leads, appointments, follow-ups, launches, and more! Everything takes too long because I need to make sure everything's done well and right. I always give a hundred times value to my clients and partners. It never ends. No matter how much I do, the work piles up, getting bigger by the day.

Later, whenever I look at my long, long list, I feel like I'm drowning. Overwhelmed. Frozen. Paralyzed. My head is buzzing. I'm physically here, but I'm not here. Time stands still yet goes so fast at the same time. I look around, but a veil seems to separate me from my surroundings. People look distant and blurry, as in a fog. The world feels muted.

Besides the piles of deadlines at work, the clutter of toys, laundry, and dishes at home begin weighing me down. My infant calls for me while my husband faults me for the growing mess. The phone rings—it's another call from my fault-finding brother. It rings again—it's my mother giving me a lecture on how to clean, cook, and serve my husband better.

All these things are machine-gun bullets flying at me, ambushing my senses, and it's all because I'm trying to have it all and do it all. I'm so spent. I want to keep going, but my fuel is all squeezed out and exhausted.

But I must keep on going. I can't let anything stop me!

Some months pass, and I find myself in bed, soaking the pillow and sheets with tears. I feel my skin burning, and it's excruciating. I glimpse at myself in the mirror, and it looks like someone got a knife and peeled my face and neck—all swollen and inflamed. The pain feels like lemon was squeezed all over it. I never imagined this happening to me. Why should I suffer like this? The doctors have diagnosed this as *a stress-related autoimmune disease that has no cure.* While muffling my cries in bed, I hear a louder screaming from the next room. Aden, my fourteen-month son, has just woken up. We've been co-sleeping and breastfeeding on demand since he was born. But this night, I have to put him in the other room with his big sister, my stepdaughter, Allyson. It's painful to hear him looking for me and wanting to nurse. But I can't.

Earlier this morning, Aden's face has turned so red, and his temperature shot up; he'd been projectile-vomiting. I had no idea the medicine I was taking would do this to him. The doctor assured me it was safe. Now it's apparent it's not!

I no longer know what's more painful—my face burning, the milk hardening in my breasts, or hearing my son crying when I couldn't get him. As tears stream from my eyes, I blow and clear my nose. What's most painful is I'm not good enough, and I'll never be good enough even if I die trying.

It makes sense that stress caused this autoimmune disease because I've been working myself to death just to prove I can do it all—making great money helping business owners grow their company and be a great mom. I recall the times when I rushed back home in between meetings to make sure my baby didn't feel abandoned, when breastmilk spilled over my work clothes because I was pumping milk while driving amid LA traffic. When a meeting ran too long, I had to endure the pain of milk hardening in my breasts. I've also been trying to prove I'm strong enough to withstand my husband's intense resentment toward me. He hates that I don't have time for him or the home and makes sure I feel it.

I wipe my tears and look around my bedroom. My husband, Drew, is right. The house is filthy, the mess growing out of hand. I don't even know how to cook or clean. (Was it my fault I grew up with maids and didn't have to learn those skills?)

Part of me resents that I now don't have the kind of household help I had growing up and that I am married to someone who terrifies me. But I'm still trying. I'm really, really trying.

Aden's crying from the next room starts to get unbearable. I have to zone out. My thoughts shift to me giving birth at home without anesthesia because I learned it was best for my baby. I breastfed on demand. I read all the books and took all the classes to be the best mom I can be. His incessant crying right now tells me I'm a failure of a mother, no matter how much I try. While choking in tears, I bury my face in the pillow and scream, "Why is it never good enough, God!"

I've done everything I was told—to be positive, fearless, hardworking, and persistent, to study, withstand all challenges, and follow what I love. I've changed myself—completely! And this is what I get? Is this just another test to prove my will and determination? It's too exhausting. I'm done with this cycle of burning out and starting over. It never ends. I have exhausted all avenues. There's no way out. It feels so much better to give up, disappear, and die.

So I fall asleep, crying in despair.

Then I wake up with Aden crying again. The medicine should be out of my body now, so I rush to get him. While cradling him in my arms, I soak in his love. Even if I really want to give up, I can't.

"God, please help me!" I pray fervently.

As if on autopilot, I browse my email. One pops up that I would normally never have noticed before. Just when I'm about to hit delete, the message feels like it's calling me, so I open it.

The program sounds airy-fairy, unlike the neuroscience-based, practical, mainstream, self-growth, and business-development material I usually immerse myself in. It's inviting me to go on a deep inner journey, and I feel a tinge of reluctance. The class is expensive, and I don't have the time. But I'm desperate—willing to try anything to free myself from suffering. I must do something I've never done before. Einstein defines insanity as "doing the same thing over and over again and expecting different results." It's time to do something different.

Just like Neo in *The Matrix*, I choose to take the red pill and unravel all the answers I am seeking.

I'm saying yes.

The next day, I find myself sitting in class in Manhattan Beach. I can't understand most of what the teacher is saying, but I stay open and willing.

Then I feel my daily life shifting. Without trying, I'm no longer reactive to the things that used to trigger me. I'm sitting in the kitchen having a conversation with Drew, and it's so evident that something is different: he's listening. This never happened. Before, he would either pretend to listen or retort with something offensive. But for some reason, this time, he's just *really* listening. I'm feeling heard. It's incredible. I want more.

A deeper inner journey begins, and I dive fully into retreat after retreat for more than two years, traveling to beautiful destinations in Hawaii, Arizona, and California. I began using the coaching techniques I used to facilitate others to help myself. I experience an intense purging of my unconscious self-sabotaging tendencies. It feels like I'm dismantling every fiber of my being, just like when a caterpillar liquefies when it enters the cocoon and loses all its previous form and identity.

From this space, I realize I've been running on an external source of fuel. I've been using dirty gasoline when this human-machine should use its built-in power plant. I was bound to break with the way I was running.

All along, I thought I was doing everything for myself to fulfill my purpose and potential. I had no idea the fuel I was running on was the unconscious need to prove to my late dad I was good enough to be loved.

That wrong fuel source led me to twist myself to perfectionism, fitting in other people's judgments, trying to do everything the right way, and needing to achieve more—all to prove I'm good enough. And nothing was ever good enough for Papa. No wonder I never felt like I was good enough in anything—not as a mom or wife, not in my business, health, and relationships.

Worse, I was never good enough for me.

I realize that the pull for *more* I felt all my life is the pull to be *more of me*. To utilize the innate power source I was designed with. To allow the natural joy, love, laughter, and bliss that every person is born with to energize every breath, moment, conversation, task, and project. To not hold back my joy and laughter for fear of offending anyone because I'm too much, too insensitive, too immature, or too unprofessional. To not hold back my voice because it might be too loud. To not hold back my energy because people might say it's too strong.

To be shamelessly me!

It's not about using my willpower to ignore judgments and criticisms, not even to reframe them as feedback or any way that would tell my mind it shouldn't matter. Those strategies are unsustainable for me. It's all about judgment no longer having a grip on me, because judgment no longer fuels me.

My true power is being me!

Once I stepped into my true power, everything began transforming. The stress-related autoimmune skin disease that's supposed to be incurable has healed. I'm now the mom I want to be. I'm possessed by joy, abundance, ease, and flow. Now I am able to do so much more in less time. I get to work with powerful entrepreneurs who are changing the world. My business is a pure, fun expression of me!

My toxic relationships changed into happy relationships—my husband, a self-proclaimed monster, transformed into my most loving, thoughtful, and supportive Prince Charming. When before we felt incompatible in any way, now I feel we're beyond compatible in every way. I didn't have to leave my marriage and find a new man. The same man I married magically changed when I chose to be me!

Hallelujah!

Time passes. Now I have two little boys. I just got home feeling high and blissful from a deeply transformational retreat. I have a huge project due in less than a week, which I've barely started since I was away. My sons miss me so much and want their mommy all the time.

My mom and sister are visiting. My brother, who I haven't been speaking to since I dared to set boundaries, has driven about seven hours straight and arrived uninvited and unannounced.

This is a perfect recipe for me to relapse into my old patterns and become *overwhelmed*.

Before, I'd already be in a panic. But this time, it's different.

My brother is angry at me as he felt hurt I didn't wake up to greet him; he threatens to leave. He starts his usual litany of hurtful words. Each word is like a spray of bullets from a machine gun.

Ratatatatat…

Back then, I'd get hit with every bullet. Now it's different. Each bullet approaches as if in slow motion. I can easily flick it with my fingers up in the air. Like in *The Matrix*.

I'm now bulletproof.

All I'm doing is just sitting here embodying love and holding him in so much love.

In mid-sentence, he pauses and says, "You seem different." I feel him soften and open up. Just like that, he stops attacking. For the first time in all our decades growing up, he stops telling me everything wrong about me. We hug and say to each other, "I love you."

My brother has magically turned into pure love right in front of my eyes, and it's all because I chose to be me.

The next day comes. It's Friday, the day for my big project launch. There are no jitters, stress, anxiety, or overwhelm like before. I'm calm, excited, blissful. I can't believe the amount of work I got done in a very short time. I even got to enjoy my kids, husband, and family visiting. It's so good how everything got done in sweet flow. I don't need to have everything figured out. I don't need to do it perfectly. It's all so fun!

After my presentation, I receive messages of praise and acknowledgment of how great it went. The money that abundantly flowed afterward is incredible.

I'm still continually in awe of the magic and miracles that happen when I choose to be in my true power. In being the love that I am, I achieve everything I seek to achieve. I get everything I ask and more. Without sacrificing or compromising. Without needing to do everything or please everyone.

I feel so blissful about my health, business, relationships, and all of me. I can now say that finally, I have true success! I'm still not perfect, just perfectly imperfect! I am happy, abundant, and free!

My Body Is My Guru
How My Body Guided
My Awakening to My True Power

Leslie Sandra Black

Pilgrimage in India

Here I am, finally on my lifelong dream of taking a pilgrimage in India to quantum-leap my spiritual awakening. I've spent two glorious, expansive weeks with the Hindu guru Amma, whom millions worldwide honor as "the hugging saint" because she lovingly embraces and blesses each person she meets.

Amma has long impressed me as one who radiantly embodies the Divine Feminine. Staying at her Amritapuri Ashram, nestled between the Arabian Sea and the Kerala Backwaters with its ornate brightly colored temple and lush tropical vegetation, was key in my calling to India. While spending two months there and in other ashrams, I gratefully received many beautiful, profound activations that fueled my spiritual awakening. This was indeed the spiritual and energetic nourishment for which I had been longing! And I glow with gratitude for all I'm deeply integrating.

I had spent decades actively supporting others, giving them my all. In my twenties and thirties, I gave twelve years to wholeheartedly supporting marginalized communities, first in the inner city, then living and working in a northern indigenous village.

For the next twenty years, I served full time as an energy healer, holistic therapist, and teacher-coach of energy healers, incredibly grateful to be transmitting Divine Love to thousands of people. During this, I also raised two amazing kids and supported my beloved spouse through his lively career and his miraculous journey through and beyond cancer. My life was inspired, purposeful, beautiful, and blessed.

As I grew into my mid-fifties, my body started complaining. I inexplicably recovered from several odd physical ailments—each time trusting my body would bounce back and continue to serve me well. I became more and more aware of an underlying exhaustion. I longed for deeply nurturing breaks from all demands on me. I had been offering myself as a "lifeline" for many people in my circles of family, clients, students, peers, community, and the wider world. I wanted to turn off my energetic HELP IS HERE sign. I wanted to clear my ever-expanding to-do lists. I also wanted to stop pushing myself to be a better, more giving person.

But I never imagined the alarming distress I would find myself in during a spiritual pilgrimage. Here I am now, shivering feverishly in a windowless concrete room in a remote town, in the mountains of Andhra Pradesh, India. Every few minutes, my belly erupts in wrenching pain, and I must dash to the bedside toilet. Constant, severe head pressure keeps me awake, day and night. All I can do between toilet trips is to consciously breathe in and out. Breathe in…breathe out… The breath holds me together physically and emotionally, moment by moment, through several long days and nights. That, and repeating aloud the activating mantra Amma gave me six weeks earlier.

I had accepted an invitation to join an NGO project in its visitations to remote subsistence tribal villages (*Adivasi*) in the Paderu region. My acceptance was my conditioned automatic response. I now know I consciously betrayed my own pilgrimage purpose of much-needed rest and renewal. With my twelve-year background of working with marginalized people in Canada, visiting these impoverished villages seemed a natural flow for me—to be with others out of compassionate presence, transmitting Divine Love and Light.

Now, mistakenly assuming my familiarity with marginalized communities, I'm shocked by this incomprehensible level of poverty and struggle. I see women fetching and carrying water from a polluted river. A bent-over, elderly woman persistently pumps her village's well to show me the resulting trickle of brown sludge. There was no rain last season for the rice paddies, and people are starving because they were duped into growing coffee instead of food crops. There's no social safety net here.

I feel the shock in my gut (interestingly known in science as our "emotional brain"). The emotional impact on me, along with unclean water, has created a powerful sucker punch to my sensitive, sanitized gastrointestinal system. I'm horrified at how my healthy body has crumbled. *Why has my strong, fit body collapsed? Why is this happening to me? I have come to India for renewal after decades of doing healing work and community service. What have I done wrong for this to happen? God, please help me!*

Amid my appalling physical and mental distress here in my Paderu room comes an answer. Arising in my awareness is an expansive Presence of Divine Light, and it's gently laughing:

"You wanted to fully awaken, my Love. So here is your cave time…dark, cold, alone, on the mountain, like the Indian rishis have done over the centuries. Except that you have been given a toilet, a locking door, water, rice, and bananas. Say your mantra. Breathe. This is your path to the 'Cave of your Heart'—that for which you have been searching. It's here now. Don't fight this."

The Cave of the Heart, in Hindu cosmology, is a spiritual space in the center of the body. Through this space, we access our own sacredness, our true power. Holy wow! This clarifying message will give me the focus to endure through unrelenting physical challenges over the next ten days, and ultimately over two years.

Continuing the pilgrimage at home

Upon my return to Canada, I feel huge resistance to jump back into the demanding pace of my pre-pilgrimage life. Gone is the former drive of pushing myself to juggle responsibilities and schedules, ensuring everyone in my world is well served. My body shows me that it requires extending my pilgrimage for a few more months—at home. My heart, filled with both joy and struggle from my four months of pilgrimage in India, reassures me that it's best to listen to my body!

My body has now literally assumed the leadership of my at-home pilgrimage. It shows me how to let go of all control—to simply allow. It shares its wisdom with me through its body language and signals. The messages it gives me are shocking and all-consuming. I've no idea of the depth of journey I've agreed to allow. My "cave time" is continuing.

First is the spreading of inflammation throughout my gastrointestinal tract, causing painful, intense cramping. The swelling spreads into my joints, face, and eyes. Copious tears stream steadily from my eyes, blurring my vision. My swelling face has aged thirty more years, and I'm losing much of my hair. Laboratory tests reveal both bacterial and parasitic infections.

My body now clearly communicates its requirement for deep rest most every day. My functional medicine doctor says my body's energy reserves are depleted, so I have no capacity to heal. If I try to push myself to do a task, I get totally drained, almost instantly. So I sleep, pray, meditate, and repeat my mantra. I allow my sympathetic nervous system to relax, unwind, and flatline, honoring my body's requirements. I allow space for integrating the many potent activations and experiences of my India pilgrimage and ashram immersions. I'm aware of the many deep spiritual teachings of the path of letting go of *doing* and letting go of external gratifications. A path of deepening into the stillness of *being*. The rishis of India did this intense practice while fasting in mountain caves. I'm *being* in stillness in the cave of my dark bedroom.

I know my body is not against me. I cannot live without it. My body led me, as a guru would, to this place because I had opened to my awakening journey. It had some wise knowing that this cave time is required for me to quantum-leap. This time of deep rest *is* the practice, journey, and path. It is not "time out" but rather "time in."

Diving deeply into the physical discomfort, I tearfully ask my body to show me what's happening to it. It shows me its depletion from decades of giving my own life force and power away to others. All my life, in both work and personal life, I had placed the others' needs ahead of mine. I remember I often had days feeling completely drained. I often wondered why my body was tired and letting me down. I had assumed, as do most of us, that my body was a machine here to serve me and obey my wishes. Now I'm finally slowed down enough to recognize that my body is conscious and has its own voice. And its messages to me are very disturbing.

My body shows me, through sensations of body memory, that this pattern of self-sacrificing began in my family of origin. I feel it like a powerful script, or a computer program, that I was given in utero. My scripted role is to serve others and ignore my own needs. Woah! I recall I was told I performed this role exceedingly well, as a "very good girl." In my childhood years during the '60s and '70s, this servant mandate was also strongly enforced outside my home—at school, at church, and in the media.

As a child for whom the presence of God was palpable, teachings about Jesus profoundly influenced me. I learned that my giving to and prioritizing others was honoring God. Jesus' sacrifice on the cross was deeply imprinted in my psyche, encouraging me to give without concern for my well-being. These programs or scripts are so deeply implanted they guided my life and choices over the decades. I pushed myself to exhaustion so many days trying to do more before going to sleep, feeling guilty and purposeless if I didn't give my all. No wonder my power drained out. Becoming aware of these deeply ingrained programs is a massive wake-up call for me!

Brain fog

After giving it all this loving rest and attention, I fully expect my body to bounce back. Instead, my energy levels are decreasing, both physically and mentally. My wise body won't allow me to override it. I must give in to this exhaustion—to unplug and flatline rest.

Communicating with others is exhausting. To engage or respond demands energy that's not available. In trying to connect with friends through texting, I discover I just cannot. My thoughts are confused and full of gaps. My mind has lost the power to string together concepts or words.

This is severe brain fog. My brain is very inflamed. Pathogens are attacking my neurons.

My world seems to be underwater…opaque water…and everything is moving slowly. Music playing in my house is painfully stimulating. It exhausts me, making demands on me to engage with it. I simply can't.

I cannot *do* anything. When preparing lunch, I drop the knife twice while cutting cucumbers, just missing my bare foot. Reaching into the fridge to pull out an egg, I knock over an uncovered dish of tomato sauce and drop the raw egg into it, on the floor. I collapse on the floor in tears. Cleaning up the mess is more than I can handle. I give up on lunch.

Trying to overcome this severe brain fog is like driving a car when the gas tank is empty. I have minimal access to my cognitive abilities. All is blurry and dull.

My quick mind is no longer my identity. If my mind is me, then I am nothing.

I'm in shock, traumatized. *How can this happen to me?* I sob. *My mind is gone. I cannot connect with the world outside of me. I'm all alone. My beautiful, loving life is gone. Less than a year earlier, I bravely leapt into my dream pilgrimage, longing to fully embody my True Self. How did that loving intention lead me to this powerless state?*

Surrender

Over several weeks in my bed cave, I have wept deeply into what the medieval mystic St. John of the Cross called the "Dark Night of the Soul." I recall the message I received in my "Paderu cave"—to not fight the body symptoms and to open to the Cave of my Heart. Now my "choiceless choice" is to let go.

I completely surrender, as into riptides of the ocean, allowing them to carry me, letting go of all struggle and grasping. I let go of all my dreams and loves, my identity and life. I surrender even my will to live—or to now die. I'm willing to go Home.

I choose to be fully in the Cave of my Heart, returning to Love, to Source.

My "monkey mind" is quiet. So incredibly quiet…and peaceful.

My sleeping and liminal hours fill with beautiful dreams, visions, and angelic Presence. My body feels lovingly held, bathing in comforting waves of love my child self never received. I welcome these gorgeous energies to gently heal my physical and emotional bodies from the wounding and abandonment of my childhood.

I notice that part of me is watching me go through these shifts. My Witness, my True Self, is now so clearly recognizable. Gone are the interfering stories and fears of my cognitive monkey mind.

As I relax into these expansive states of Presence and Peace, I realize I'm now truly *being* in the sublime Cave of my Heart. This is the Peace that passes all understanding.

Living from my Heart

The brain fog lasted in diminishing degrees for two years. This has given me time to observe the dissonant vibration my returning cognitive mind brings into my Heart space. They are two distinctly different aspects of me, and it's now easy to distinguish between them! This realization, much more than just a silver lining to my dark cloud, is the Great Gift of my pilgrimage!

During meditation times, I now easily enter expansive, nonlinear states of consciousness. Flow states of my Heart feel so nourishing and loving as I sink into them ever more eagerly.

While meditating, I ask Presence if there's more I can glean from this extended pilgrimage. I hear a friendly voice say to me:

"You asked to awaken on your pilgrimage! Well, honey, you needed more than the four months you planned in India! In the Indian ashrams, you were activated. Your pilgrimage integration continued back home where your body could finally rest. Your wise body sacrificed its wellness to stop you sacrificing yourself through your *serving and doing*. It was your *guru* guiding you to allow your True Being to lead your life. Your cognitive mind had a strong grip on you. Now you are accessing, through your Heart, who you truly are—a Being far beyond the limitations of your mind!"

Life after pilgrimage

The brain fog has completely cleared! My body is healthy! In joyful celebration, my beloved spouse and I are vacationing on the gorgeous island of Maui. I'm fully present, absorbing the exquisite beauty of the hibiscus and the tall palms off our patio. Breathing in the warm tropical scents of plumeria and yummy coconut inspires me to breathe ever more deeply. While sauntering along the beautiful beaches, hiking in the lush jungle, exploring enchanting lava fields, my body delights in feeling returned strength and buoyant life force energies. My full immersion into the clear, warm ocean is the embrace of pure Love. I delight in the accompaniment of the endearing sea turtles and the multicolored sea life in the coral reefs. I choose to live immersed in the sea of loving, supportive Presence. I notice, for the first vacation ever, that I'm not mentally processing, striving to improve myself or be on a quest for answers.

I attentively listen to when and how my body wants to move, play, or rest. As I notice tension in my back, I interrupt whatever I'm doing to gently stretch, following the lead of my muscles. Overriding my body's requirements is no longer an option for me. I've quit forcing food into my upset belly in the morning. As I eat breakfast near noon, my gut, which has endured such intense distress, is now calm and relaxed. Through muscle testing, I ask my body, not my mind, what food it prefers. My gut lining has totally healed as I avoid eating inflammatory foods such as wheat, corn, and dairy. My wise guru body feels clear and flowing— immensely grateful it no longer bears separation within me. It joyfully embodies my Being, my true power! I feel so much gratitude for its tough-love wise Guidance!

Back home, my cognitive mind seems grateful to function once again, with a much lighter, more appropriate workload, with clarity rather than confusion. There are few demands on it during my coaching and energy healing sessions with clients, as wisdom flows readily through my Heart. Foundational to my thoughts and emotions is a vibration of peace, as I live in alignment with Being—in my true power.

I delight in my transformational sessions with my clients! I no longer feel exhausted as I've stopped giving away my personal life force. No longer am I affected by the pain-body of my clients. My Heart now transcends the dimensions of such separation. I notice that infinite

Source pours through me clearly, powerfully, and I am inspired by the loving energies that speak through my voice!

As I BE the true power of Love and Light within myself, Source energy becomes available wherever I focus. I choose to be a fully embodied *lighthouse*, guiding others to find their way home to their own true power. It's such relief to have eradicated the former self-destructive *lifeline* program. I sense that such a program was implanted long ago and has run in me for many lifetimes. My body, my heart, and my divine Being have now turned self-sacrifice on its head! Paradoxically, self-love and self-honoring bestow true power on myself and others!

My life now flows with ease and overflowing delight! This is divinely beautiful living and loving. I'm eternally grateful to my own body for acting as the guru that guided me into awakening to the true power in my Heart.

Fearlessly Unstoppable

Suyen Angbetic Bailey

Growing up in the tropical island of Cebu, Philippines, I love playing outdoors from morning till dusk, climbing up trees, picking up flowers, riding my bike, hitting the beach, watching beautiful sunsets, and going with Big Mama, my paternal grandmother, to Ateliers for *terno* fittings. A *terno* is a Filipino formal gown with butterfly sleeves. Fascinated by the artistry and process of making a garment, I watch the ladies sew every bead or pearl into the cloth by hand while the designer checks the embroidery. I dream of being a fashion designer when I grow up.

It's August of 1982. I arrive in the US, the land of opportunity. As I look out the car window, I see a magnificent sunset. It makes me smile and fills my heart with hope of my new journey in a foreign land. It's a dream come true for me to study fashion design here. Then I move from Los Angeles to the fashion capital of the world, New York City. There I had my first sight of snowflakes falling from the sky with ease and grace. So pure and heavenly! It's in this alluring city that never sleeps, the Big Apple, where I met my ex-husband, a tall, slim, charming, and handsome Irish man from the Midwest.

With majors in advertising and journalism, he manages a newspaper in the city. I see him approaching me. "Here are the issues that you ordered," he says and hands them to me. "Can I show you something real quick?"

In my mind, I am asking, *Why is he trying to sell me space in the paper?* No sale happens, but he manages to get my phone number! Then he calls and invites me to a restaurant opening. Nope, he just wants to sell me something.

Two weeks later, he invites me to a Broadway show. Hmm, sounds appealing, but I politely decline. The third try is another invitation to an opening party. I'm starting to get flattered but do not want to think anything of it. He meets models, actresses, and people in show business because of his job, so why me? He's persistent. He read that Filipinos are Catholics, so he calls and asks, "Suyen, where do you attend mass? I will be attending mass too. Can we meet at church?"

I say yes without hesitation. I meet friends at church all the time. We attend mass at St. Patrick's Cathedral, our first date. A refined gentleman, very soft-spoken, reserved, with great table manners, and extremely charming while talking about New York City. He looks so dashing in that scarf while I figure out the color of his eyes. He pulls my chair as I stand up to go to the powder room. *Is this real?*

We are about to leave, and no sales pitch has happened. I'm keeping my composure, but my heart is pounding inside. I think he likes me. This is insane.

He wants to go out with me again. I'm delighted like a naive schoolgirl. I had attended an all-girls Catholic school from kindergarten to college and never had a boyfriend. Now I know what it feels like to be swept off my feet!

I'm living the dream working as an assistant fashion designer for a Korean evening wear company on Seventh Ave., the Fashion Ave. of the Americas, and having a whirlwind relationship with a handsome Prince Charming in New York City. I'm sitting in the back of a long stretch limo he'd sent to pick me up to attend an off-Broadway show he'd produced. I'm enjoying my ride as we pass by dazzling skyscrapers, museums, Broadway theatres, restaurants, iconic landmarks, etc. What an interesting and diverse city, a kaleidoscope of nationalities!

Our dates are mesmerizing, from dining at fancy five-star restaurant openings and going to Broadway shows, movies, parks, off-Broadway shows, to ball games at Shea and Yankee stadiums. Since I always wear high heels, he buys me rubber shoes. Yup, need to pick up my speed, or I'd get run over by New Yorkers! It's more comfortable now that I'm pregnant.

After a year of being married, I realize I made a mistake. My religious beliefs, culture, and the hope that things will change for the better are reasons why I keep giving him many chances. He's not the Prince Charming I thought he was. He's more of a Jekyll and Hyde, with a bad unpredictable temper. He once told his officemate that he likes to date Asian women because they make good slaves. I grew up in the Philippines with help, no real chores, or household work. Am I qualified to be a slave?

I wash his wool and cashmere sweaters and shrink all of them into children's size while his shirts turn pink. I recall during the early years of marriage how his eyeballs almost popped out in disbelief when I was cooking. The oil was flying all over the counters, walls, floor, and even around me. I flooded our kitchen floor, broke some stuff, and I cooked food that ended in the trash. I learn fast and consider myself a well-trained "slave." I do my best, but my best is never good enough. I'm always careful how I say and do things for fear of angering him. It's like walking on eggshells, constantly being criticized, yelled at, humiliated, and blamed for his unacceptable behavior. He can't fathom how his wife from a third-world country can't do household work like his mother who raised six boys.

He comes home at 2:00 a.m. I hear him walking to the bedroom. I'm horrified, wondering what mood he's in. I smell alcohol, pot, and cigarette smoke. I pretend to be asleep, my heart pounding against my chest. He pulls the blanket, picks me up from the collar of my pajamas, and throws me on the bed. He does it again, again, and again. I feel like a rag doll or in a Space Mountain ride in Disneyland.

I have to twist my body away from the edge of the bed. I'm afraid I will hit my head at the sharp corner of the side table. It could be fatal! He slaps me so hard, and I fall on the warm blue carpet. Numb all over my body, I try to wiggle my toes and fingers with no success. He cries and apologizes, "I am sorry, you do not deserve this." I could not feel the ice on my face.

Am I paralyzed? Am I having a brain hemorrhage? Am I going to die? I'm still totally numb! Why not call 911? This is it! I'm extremely scared, angry, sad, hopeless, and traumatized. Is this what I deserve for not being a good slave? Please, God, help me! I have children to take care of!

Looking back, it started with verbal abuse that escalated to throwing stuff at me, spitting, pinching, pulling my hair, pushing, slapping, and even hitting me when I was seven months pregnant with our second child. I end up with bruises and a black eye. It's very shocking and confusing to me. How can someone have so much anger? This only happens in the movies! I feel so alone and isolated miles away from home, family, and friends, but I don't want to tell them so they won't worry. My dream of becoming a fashion designer? So close, yet so far! I'm now a failure and losing my zest for life.

Sitting at the edge of the bed, I'm crying, feeling depressed, stupid, unappreciated, and worthless. The pain is too much to handle. Life is unbearable, and I want to give up! Then I see my five-year-old daughter and four-year-old son in front of me. How long have they been standing there? I wonder. I look into their big brown eyes and feel their sadness, confusion, and fear. I'm so overcome with sadness myself, but out of embarrassment, guilt, and shame. That shakes me up to the core. How can I even think of giving up? My children need me! They need a strong, healthy, and responsible mother. Despite having a broken heart and wounded spirit, I wipe my tears, put on a brave smile, and tell them I will always be there for them. We snuggle in bed together. I want them to feel safe and secure with me. Truth is, they are the ones giving me strength and courage. My children are my inspiration and motivation to never give up and always thrive in life.

He wants to save our marriage, so we move to Chicago, then to the Bay Area in California years later. The physical abuse stops after we leave New York while the verbal and psychological abuse continues on and off. Our relationship is like a roller-coaster ride filled with different levels of ups and downs, twists and turns at different speeds. It can be encouraging, fun, exciting, scary, nerve-wracking, joyful, calming, intense, disappointing, hopeful. Life in California is like a huge roller-coaster ride. It has many exhilarating turns with short dips, then there's the pause, the amazing feeling of being on top of the world before the huge drop. Hold on tight! The big fall is coming. Then the crash!

Unfortunately, my ex is having a relapse of his abusive behavior. His best friend and boss committed suicide. That throws him into a downward spiral; he begins drinking, gambling, falling into depression and anger. He isn't willing to seek help as I suggested. I feel bad, but I cannot help someone who's not willing.

It's a beautiful morning. From our kitchen garden window, I'm watching the hummingbirds go from one flower to another as I check the new blooms of different colored roses in our three-tiered rose garden. The children are all home. As we prepare breakfast, my daughter says, "Mom, you should get a divorce." The other two concur and express their support. Did they read my mind? I've been contemplating it for months. Immensely fearful, my mind is spinning with uncertainty and countless questions. What will my life be like after the divorce? Will I survive being on my own? I put my career/dream aside and make the children my priority. What if staying is better instead of facing the unknown? On the other hand, I do not want my children to think it's all right to stay in a bad relationship. Life is too short not to be happy. I desire to be strong for the children, but I have to be strong for me now.

At forty-eight and after twenty-one years of marriage, I let go and let God—total surrender! My ex agrees to the divorce but wants to wait till after our anniversary on July 4. What a perfect day to get my independence back! I got married and lost my independence on Independence Day!

Living separate lives under one roof for two years, I nurture and heal my bruised spirit through reading self-help material and attending intensive boot camp–style transformational programs like going through obstacle courses, walking on glass, crossing from one tree to another at thirty feet high, etc. I get myself certified in coaching and in different healing modalities to heal myself and build my self-esteem. I prepare myself to be *fearless* and *unstoppable* like I'm going into battle—the "Divorce and the Big Unknown Battlefields."

Divorce is challenging for everyone, but we manage to move on. I meet Steve, my current husband, two years after the divorce. I'm very apprehensive at first; nonetheless, we hit it off immediately! Barely interested in getting into another relationship, I resist, but my gut feeling tells me, "Long term, and a nice man." I feel comfortable, safe, and secure with him. He has a level of maturity I admire. On our first dinner date, I notice he's nervous. Totally not pretentious—what you see is what you get! "Where have you been?" he asks. "You are the woman of my dreams!" He mentions marriage early. No longer a naive schoolgirl, I'm flattered, but not swept off my feet this time!

"I would love my friends to meet you," he says. "I'm lucky to have wonderful and supportive female friends. They check on me all the time, especially now that I'm going through a divorce and my mom has stage-4 cancer. One calls every day at 8:00 a.m. to ask how I'm doing."

"That's awesome," I respond to Steve. "I can't wait to meet them!"

The door opens, and his friends welcome us with big smiles.

"What do you want to drink, Suyen? Red wine, white, gin, soda?"

"I don't drink. I'll have water, thank you!" I say and notice one great female friend he mentions seems distant. Holding a glass of wine, she looks at me from head to toe. She gives me "the look." If looks could kill, I'd be dead by now. Okay, she's a protective friend, understandable! A few months later at a Christmas party, another female very close to him gives me "the look" again. Extremely more potent than the previous one. After the third, fourth, and so on, I have gotten used to "the look."

Being sensitive to energy and after several get-togethers, I discern how he is sought after by his female friends. I realize people in his circle are not thrilled about us being together. To my dismay, his female friends in their fifties and sixties are like women from the Golden Girls acting like *Mean Girls* in high school. Two-faced, with their schemes, lies, intimidation, rudeness to my face.

Just to give you a picture, one whispers into my ear and says, "Take care of my man." Meaning Steve. Another says, she can lie and do anything, and Steve will believe her, as they've known each other for the longest time. Then there's his ex who seems to have an informer; she calls and leaves him messages whenever we travel. There's also an entitled manipulative realtor who has no respect for boundaries. Is there some kind of initiation or list I am missing? No intention of cutting in front of anyone. Just being myself—an Asian with a strong accent!

Yet he blindly defends them, saying, "They are my friends and would never do such things." He tells me more, "You are playing games, making up stories, jealous, and controlling."

It hurts to be accused of things resulting from his friends' schemes. His loyalty to them is very admirable, though. The arrows might be targeted at me, but it's his psyche they are messing with. They're just plain cruel, insensitive, and selfish. They are betraying him, and I feel betrayed myself—not by them, but by him. Does he really not know his friends? Is he in denial? I feel taken for granted, disrespected and unsupported. This is neither the relationship I want nor deserve. I'm leaving him after his mom joins our Creator. I have a special bond with his mother. I go with them to her treatments twice a week for two and a half years unless I'm travelling. Steve and I see her almost every day, then every day in her last months. It's during this difficult time that we notice qualities in each other we admire. Extremely devoted and committed, he's a great son. These traits are commendable! As the saying goes, "the truth always comes out in the end." He finally witnesses his two-faced friends treat me with disrespect. One by one, layer by layer, the truths about his "friends" unravel.

Distraught, he asks for my forgiveness for the first time in three years: "I am so sorry, Suyen, for not believing you and giving them the benefit of the doubt. Please do not leave. I want our relationship to work."

I feel his pain and sincerity. We do love each other. Love is the invisible thread that connects both of us amidst the storms. Love is power from within. There's also tremendous power in forgiveness; it bridges hurt and pain to healing and growth.

Steve and I are now married for seven years and together for eleven. Coming from different backgrounds, beliefs, and cultures, there is never a dull moment. Despite our differences, we share common interests that make life interesting, exciting, and adventurous. I remember him asking me on our first dinner date, "Suyen, do you get seasick?"

I replied, "No, I grew up traveling by boat several times a year to different islands in the Philippines." I pass the seasickness test, and we enjoy bringing *Super*, his fifty-foot yacht to Catalina Island every summer. Our weekend getaway! We also savor different kinds of food especially during our travels abroad. I have great passion for travel, art, history, learning about different cultures and mingling with locals. One thing we both love to do is catching the sunset wherever we are, from the different US states to countries in Asia, Central and South America, Western and Eastern Europe, Caribbean Islands, Tahiti, Bora Bora, etc.

Grateful and blessed, I feel like dreaming in a new dawn every day. Moving from California to Florida is a dream come true for Steve. As avid boaters, we relish cruising up and down the Intracoastal Waterways. It's extremely blissful and enjoyable to feel the breeze on my face while he's on top of the world driving the boat and riding the waves. We are surrounded by water, boats, and nature as we bathe in the magnificent sunset from our new home.

"Know thyself" and "love thyself" are truths that I consistently remind myself after years of not being able to stand up for myself. It is not just important to know but "to be." Love is my Inner True Power and all that is. My unending quest for the truth, self-realization, and transformation continues.

As I watch the sunset in its magnificent power, I see a reflection of my Fearless and Unstoppable self. Just like sunsets, "I AM" God's magnificent creation!

Living a Life of Freedom

Judith Krug

I'm a daughter of the Hungarian Freedom Fighters, who escaped before the Russians could arrest them. You may have seen some historical pictures of that 1956 Hungarian Revolution. While students in America were singing Elvis's song "All Shook Up," Hungarian students had started a revolution against the Russian occupation.

Tanks came rolling down the streets, like Tiananmen Square in China, but it was like a freeway of tanks throughout Hungary. Those brave enough to throw Molotov cocktails at the tanks and that somehow made it out alive had no choice but to escape, many over the Austrian border.

My parents were part of that student protest, lucky enough to escape to New Jersey. Today, you may ask, why New Jersey? Why not Paris? I could have been giving this talk in French if they did, or not talking at all, just expressing myself in painting or as some sultry Parisian singer.

In 1957, New Jersey was a nice place, with lots of dairy farms and vegetable farms to feed New York. At least it didn't have tanks rolling down the streets. Like the many immigrants before them, they wanted the opportunity and freedom America announced with the beautiful Lady keeping the light on in the New York harbor.

Though I'm born in America, my parents are proud of their Hungarian heritage. I spoke only Hungarian till I was five. The culture shock of kindergarten wasn't buffered by any sibling: I'm an only child. You could say I'm hungry to fit in and be liked. This is my American experience, which is probably the same for most immigrant children.

Of course, I also want to please my parents and make them proud. This is especially true for my father, who avoids my mom and me with his obsession to build his company. My mother is the primary person to please because she has to prove to my father that she's doing a great job in raising their only daughter. There was a whole lot of pleasing going on for a guy who was hardly present. I learned English quickly and became hyper-alert to the needs of those around me to make sure I could fit in.

Playing with the other kindergartners, I learned the basic social dynamics of "who's in and who's out" and all the lying and hiding games. Those lessons have carried over throughout my schooling. I learned to blend naturally in that social fabric, as a chameleon would in its surroundings. Though I spent much of my time at home with my Hungarian culture, my education was teaching me to adjust to a culture outside and switch up my game. I was always the "good girl."

As a teen, I started to rebel against what I could feel was being expected of me, and I set some goals for myself. I convinced my mother that modeling school would be a good way of getting started in my American life. She agreed—a sort of a miracle. She was always old-school and overprotective. In many ways, modeling school embodied her old-world concept of finishing school, where the nobility in Hungary would send their daughters before sending them out in the world to get a good "catch." At that time, the Hungarian culture and the American culture for women were pretty much about getting the man who would define your life. She wants the very best for me.

To her surprise, I soon began working in Manhattan as a fashion model. I enjoy the photographic experience that celebrates my being a woman, and I like the approval I get from my agency and from work in general. With modeling, I realize the work is not about my being a human coat hanger for the clothing as much as it's about the energy I'm exuding by my Presence.

When my hairdresser tells me about the EST enlightenment classes, I become curious and sign up.

EST deeply impressed me, for it allowed me to easily transform some core ideas about myself. It isn't about getting distracted by pleasing others. My little chameleon world is about to get rocked, and I really love rock and roll. I'm ready to be rocked by EST.

I become obsessed with the deeper meanings of life, and EST is taking me there. I begin assisting in many programs. I share my transformation with my parents, and my father believes I've joined a communist cult that had me working for the "Party" for nothing. As a die-hard anti-communist, he feels I must have been brainwashed to be working without a paycheck. To control the situation, he takes my car away. I'm still defiant, so he stops paying my tuition. When I tell him he could do nothing to stop my path to enlightenment, he says:

"Well, life is what I have given you and that is the life I can take away."

At that moment, he becomes "my Russia." I know I need to flee the home that he now declares as his territory. He's rolling in the tanks; I'm now the Freedom Fighter thinking how to escape with my life.

That same night, I arrange with my friend to drive up to my street with another friend for support. As soon as they honk the horn, I take my two packed bags and run downstairs.

My mother, who's heard me packing, knows what's about to happen. As she sees me coming out of my room with my bags, she runs and barricades the door. But I push her out of the way to get to the getaway car. My friends start to drive away, casually celebrating my escape till they see my father running out of the house and me ducking down in the back seat. At that point, they gun it—with my father running after the car.

This is my first great escape.

It's also my first great insight: there's a cost to being dependent in this world.

*

Escaping from my father might have made me a rebel, but one never does escape confronting oneself. The exploration that began with EST continues through college. I take up Business Administration at Seton Hall

University and pay for the degree with my modeling jobs.

At the university, I meet a brilliant professor named Dr. Michael Valente, who created a weekend seminar called "Relationshop." It delves into the dynamics of love, sex, and relationships. I'm not interested in repeating the pitfalls of my parents' relationship. I want to take responsibility for my life and be a giver of what I believe is the real energy of love. When Dr. Valente moves to California to teach a yearlong course in metaphysical philosophy, I'm eager to go to take that course. I convince five friends to move with me, and I begin working with Dr. Valente to enroll students.

I love the beaches and the freedom of the California lifestyle. It's as if the song "Everything Is Beautiful" is written just for me. During that yearlong course, I meet and date Robert, my future husband. He's insistent, madly in love in a wash of metaphysical philosophy, so we put words into action and got married. One of my best friends, Clark (who left New York to join me in California), ministered us. With friends like that, you just have to love life.

Robert and I go on to start a multilevel marketing company selling Swedish health products. We're very successful, traveling the world and doing what we love. We're blessed with a baby boy, Berek, and it seems like life couldn't get any better. Then our Swedish supplier decides to go to direct sales, and we lose our business overnight. We were good at running our business, so we team up with a partner on another multilevel marketing company, who then took our business right out from under us.

We're successful at making businesses work, but there was a side to business that doesn't fit into our metaphysical meaning of life. I begin to question life's meaning and purpose. Then Clark, my best friend, dies. I was shocked by seeing his young dead body, I started to do a much deeper soul-searching. My husband is still in shock from losing two businesses.

Clark had a group of friends that believed in starting a church that promoted one's individual relationship with God. Spirituality and Clark's vision then became my life's focus. I deeply want to be around Clark's group of friends, as if to show my loyalty to him. That connection to Clark seems to deepen when the group does ecstasy together. As the group's sacramental use of ecstasy and ganja pulled me toward them, I'm losing touch with my family.

I truly feel there's a spiritual side of life that has been missing and is being given a broader purpose in the group. My new focus for my business skills was to sustain the group financially. When the group leader decided to move the group to the Florida Keys, I use my credit cards to make that happen. When she decided to set up our church in Haiti, I'm all in with the vision to help the government there become the first county to surrender to God. In my mind, I feel and see the poverty and the humility of the people, and my heart just opens to them. I don't think anyone who could witness firsthand the beauty of the energy those people expressed could not fall in love with them. My heart was gushing. As a person in charge of the cash flow, I just want some of that flow to reach them. I must have stood out like a billboard that said, "I am here to be used."

The homes that I've set up in Florida are going into foreclosure, and our funds are now next to nothing. I have tapped out all my credit cards, and I'm made to feel it's all my fault. When my new family now relocated to Haiti, I feel justified in becoming a modern-day Robin Hood. I begin writing bad checks for essential things to ship to Haiti till I'm caught and charged. Fortunately, I'm put on probation, and I convinced my probation officer that my family needs me in California.

Robert welcomes me back to live with him; though we no longer think of ourselves as husband and wife, he still respects me as a friend and the mother of our son.

That's my second great escape.

It's my second great insight: there's a cost to having people dependent on you, especially when you enable their lack of responsibility by taking it on yourself.

*

Although I'm working again, I send two hundred dollars a week to help the family in Haiti that I still feel responsible for. That's a testament to the cult leader's ability to use my guilt and empathy with the poor in Haiti to influence my life, though I thought I've already escaped. On her recommendation, I check on her ex-boyfriend, Art.

He confides in me that he wants to quit drinking and doing drugs. He's the perfect one to save and make my life meaningful to the group again. I convince

Robert to allow Art to stay, and he agrees if Art sobers up and changes his life. As Art stays sober, we form a relationship that lasts a few years living with Robert in his house.

Eventually, the cult leader comes to Robert's house, being jealous of the relationship Art and I had formed. She convinces Robert that it's not right for Art and the mother of his son to be living together in the same house.

Art and I move out. As if that isn't enough to convince me that this woman isn't my friend and doesn't have any good intentions, Art and I decide to fly to Haiti and consider moving there for good to carry on the work I believed was my calling. So again, I put my common sense and integrity aside, selling everything to get to Haiti.

It doesn't take long for the cult leader to decide that I'm not complying with the rules. I'm isolated and put into silent meditation. After feeding me with polluted water and making me violently ill, they kick me out of the group.

Art and I move back to LA and camp out for almost a year while we let nature heal me. We're able to get an apartment later, thanks to a loan from my father. Art starts fixing cars, and I sell them.

We live happily, and I give birth to our daughter, Julia. Art is sober now for about ten years.

Robert's dad has an opening in his real estate company, and I'm invited to work as an escrow officer. That's where I learned the skills for my present career. Life is perfect again.

With my new job comes longer working days, and Art has more time on his hands than he does work. His insecurity kicks in, and when his mom is diagnosed with cancer, he allows a Buddhist priest to convince him that smoking drugs was a more natural, safer high.

I'm working, making good money, and still looking for Art's love, so it's easy for me to enable his habit. I eventually join in his addiction myself.

Then I see people losing their minds at parties. Nothing about it makes sense for me. I don't want this example for my children. When my son writes me a letter after taking a class called "The Miracle of Love," it opens my heart and mind to my self-destruction. With a regained sense of courage, I wean myself off the drugs and go through a process of releasing all the sadness, grief, anger, and pain I haven't allowed myself to feel.

Art isn't willing to make the changes in his life at this time, so my daughter and I move out to another house we've both chosen. It's the love of my children that gives me the courage to find my true Spirit. If they have not given up on me, I'm not going to give up on me or allow their mother to be a role model of abuse.

The real estate market crashes in 2007, but that doesn't stop me from setting up my business. But it's not easy. The real estate market has an ebb and flow to it that leaves me wondering how I would ever survive it.

When I'm at a low point, my friend Ben takes me to an evening introductory workshop with Rikka Zimmerman. As I do her work, I simply get in touch with my inner knowing Self. From the guidance of my inner knowing Self, I feel a deep, profound love that overwhelms me with the appreciation for who I am. I feel a positive energy that couldn't be bothered by any negative emotions that I've built in the past. With that clarity, I feel a freedom, which allows me to be honest with myself and not be needy for approval from anything outside my inner knowing Self.

I naturally love the simple dance that consisted of my asking and then receiving the guidance to act on. It's like I have never learned to breathe properly, and now I'm simply breathing without "thinking."

I'm free from the dependence of seeking other's approval, to get their judgment on how to live up to their idea of what I should do to be good. I'm also free from judging them and myself, which frees me from my limitations and doubts. Soon my business begins tripling, and that abundance becomes my natural state no matter what the ebb and flow of the business world may be. My integrity is not up for negotiation whether others are bothered by it or not.

This is my third great escape.

This is my third great insight: there's no cost for the integrity of my inner abundance that I already possess.

I need only to ask for guidance from my inner knowing Self, which gives me freedom from codependency.

*

The True Power in my life lies in my ability to immensely love and stay in my presence. In this present state, I continue to express and live in gratitude. Love takes over and brings about the best results. Living in gratitude brings even more blessings.

My True Power manifests in my life by the beautiful balance within me that helps me manage my multimillion-dollar real estate financing company, Equity Funding Source, Inc. here in LA. My company is a mortgage brokerage firm that specializes in private money equity loans helping buyers and homeowners set up nonconforming equity-based loans funded by private investors. I balance the needs of my clients with the needs of my investors, which involves communication and establishing trust that all mutual needs will be met.

Rather than being codependent on others' needs, I work in a positive way to facilitate working relationships that enable others to achieve their financial goals. I help with developing inner-city housing and commerce. This gives me a daily uplifting satisfaction and fulfills my purpose to be of service. This service is possible because my inner balance expresses my confidence, ability to thrive, and resilience in challenging times.

With my freedom from codependency, I can make the right choices from my inner guidance. With making the right choices, I gain my honor and self-respect and avoid abuse. Letting go of judgments allows me to be more conscientious in my relationships. As I'm more conscientious, I'm happier because I'm not seeking others' approval. I'm not acting out of fear that I will lose their love. I have the freedom to say "yes" or "no." This freedom allows me not to fear any decision from my honest, open heart. With my open heart, gratitude naturally becomes incorporated into my family life and the happiness I experience with my children and grandchild. I'm grateful and express gratitude daily for my awesome life.

PART 2

STEPPING INTO YOUR TRUE POWER

Beauty Is a State of Being

Silvia Rios

It's a sunny spring day in Argentina. I can smell the Jacaranda trees and feel the sun shining in that warm afternoon. However, my seven-year-old mind is busy, in a hurry to get home to look at myself in the mirror.

Earlier that day at school, we had a rehearsal for the year end celebration. I'm participating in a dancing sketch. My partner is a cute, blondish boy named Carlos. He has a pair of hazel-brown eyes, a freckled face, and a big smile to go with it. He's the first boy I've ever liked.

"Carlitos is so *guapito*. I think I have a crush on him!" I say to my classmate.

"Who? The big-nosed girl?" Carlitos says to her later when he found out about it. I know that because my classmate has told me more about Carlitos reaction. And his lack of interest.

I'm a bit surprised. I don't really understand what he means. He won't even look at me.

I arrive home and drop my books at the entrance. I run to the bathroom and take a good look at myself in the mirror. *What's wrong with my nose that made Carlitos reject me?*

And he was right. My nose was too big for my face, but more than anything, it had a hump. I wish it was straight, but it is not.

That's the moment I learned to dislike my face and find fault with how I looked. That disapproval made me judge myself more and made me think I am ugly. My confidence is gone. I keep asking myself, "How could I fix this? What do I need to do to make it better? Why did God do this to me?"

My mom then tries to console me, but she can't help. Unlike me, she's beautiful, fair-skinned, with dark blond hair and green eyes. I look like my dad. I share with my mom about what happened today.

"*Hija*, when you were born, you were so dark and chubby, and your hair is black…," she begins to say.

From the look of her face and tone of her voice, it's obvious there's nothing beautiful or cute about me even when I was a baby. I can sense that my mom is worried and disappointed.

"I used to sit by the window during the full moon nights touching your nose and praying that God could make you prettier," she goes on.

That's when I started sinking in guilt and shame. *I disappointed Mama and caused her pain and shame because I don't look like her. If I looked like her, then probably she would love me more.*

As I'm dealing with these feelings caused by being ugly, my niece is born. My mother was previously married to a Sicilian man, and they had a son who was twenty years older than me.

My niece enters this world, and she's born with fair skin, curly dark hair, and green eyes—like my mom's.

Unlike me, she's really beautiful! And everybody adores her! That's when my young mind began to tell me that beauty equals love and acceptance; if beauty is not present, then love has to be earned, often the hard way. I consistently try to get my mother's approval by doing things for her and trying to make her proud.

My mom tries to ease my insecurities by encouraging me to study and prepare myself to be independent—which means to be alone too. She's proud I was a smart girl, and she says that studying would guarantee my well-being even if I could not find a husband.

My father is working as a fashion designer. He creates beautiful and colorful dresses and makes me model for him while telling me how beautiful I look, how beautiful my skin is, how well-proportioned my body is. A part of me believes it—but not for long, as my mother's lack of approval is stronger than the validation I receive from my dad.

I continue with my life focusing on studying and learning. I was blessed with an inborn curiosity, so every new thing would create a lot of enthusiasm in my world. I learned to speak different languages, play the piano, and create clothing designs for myself and my dolls. The pain of rejection makes me more compassionate toward others, and I do not judge people by how they look. I have a constant desire to do more, learn more, and excel at everything I do.

In my twenties, I start working as a scrub nurse in the operating room. There I met a student who had a nose job done in one of the hospitals run by the government. She looks good. Her surgery is free, and she recommends her surgeon to me.

I schedule a consultation with the surgeon and decide to have the surgery done. The only expense would be the pre-op pictures and some supplies. I had a modest income, and it would never cross my mind to spend money on that kind of surgery because it was seen as something superficial, and people with my background would not do such a thing.

The day of the surgery, as I'm lying on the table waiting for the procedure, the surgeon greets me from the door and then turns away and yells, "You do the nose, and I will do the eyes."

I realize he was talking to another surgeon, and I was "the nose." I'm anxious that he would not be performing the surgery. This is the doctor recommended to me, and how is it that he's not going to operate on me? It makes me feel unimportant, diminished, and rejected.

I get up from the operating table and try to leave, but the nurse holds me back and calls the doctor. So he comes back to the room and agrees to do the surgery.

Having my nose done has given me a sense of security to be around people without feeling less than them. I enjoy being photographed and feel any angle is perfect. I never feel I have a bad hair day because every day is a perfect face day!

Still, despite the successful surgery, I spend so many years of my life depressed and feeling unloved. I was also unable to be there for my beloved when I was needed most; my brother went into bankruptcy, my mother had cancer, and I could only offer my shell of a self because, deep down, I feel incomplete and broken. I look for help from psychologists. While that saved me from committing suicide, it did not help me heal from my suffering.

I stop believing in religion. The apparent security from my nose job was short-lived. I still feel incomplete inside.

About three years later, it gets worse. I'm still working as a scrub nurse in the operating room. After the first surgery for the day, I step inside the locker room and take off my mask. That's when I noticed a strange sensation in my nose. I immediately look for a mirror. The reflection shows me that my nose appears looser—its shape has changed! I'm shaking in fear, trying to convince myself that it's all just an illusion. But no, something is really wrong, and I know it as I look at my nose in the mirror.

The surgeon has performed a technique on me that did not allow the tip of the nose to stay in position for long. I'm angry at myself for having the surgery done, for the doctor wasn't maybe paying attention to me as he did not intend to operate on me that day.

I had put a lot of hope in the fact that by having a nicely shaped nose, I would be loved and accepted and happily ever after with my Prince Charming.

When I realize that my nose has collapsed, I'm devastated. All my feelings of unworthiness rise up from within me and seize me again. I feel once more that nobody will want to have a relationship with me. Then I recall the many times I have suffered from being rejected by people as well as the times I have to step away and let others take the center stage. Without beauty, I won't be anything worthy of anyone's attention. Not worthy to even look at.

The pain of comparing myself to others and always seeing that distorted image that only reflected ugliness and not measuring up has all brought me down the hole of depression yet again.

Fixing it is, financially, a big challenge. It's ironic too because every day I see women transform into beauties before my eyes, and I can't afford it.

One day, I'm assisting Dr. Sarrabayrouse in a rhinoplasty procedure. Before he stepped out of the operating room when he was finished, I lower my face mask and ask him what he thought of my nose and the technique that was used.

He's horrified and explained to me about the technique and why he would not use that approach even though he did not want to say anything bad about a colleague. He explains to me he does a different technique, and if he were to do my surgery, he would have to do a reconstruction adding cartilage from my ear. I ask him if he would be interested in helping me, and he says he would. I ask about his fees, and he says that considering I was working there, he would only charge for a donation of a certain amount in dollars.

I tell him that when I could get the money, I would do it. It would take me a couple of months to save up for that, but eventually, I'm able to do it.

In those days, most surgeries are performed under local anesthesia, so when the anesthetic infiltrates the tissue, it would cause it to swell, and sometimes the surgeon could not have a good reference of how much is swelling and how much is the scar tissue.

A week later, I return for a follow-up appointment, and the doctor is happy because the reconstruction looks good, but the shape of the nose needs improvement.

I ended up with the same nose I had before the first surgery; with the cartilage in, it was bigger; with the scar tissue, it had a hump.

Both the surgeon and I are disappointed. I go back to the operating room to have some of the scar tissue removed, but the doctor says if he puts too much anesthesia, he would have the same problem. He did his best, but I couldn't tolerate the pain of having those cuts without enough anesthesia.

After this second surgery, as frustrated as I am, I make a choice to let go of my expectations. I am trying so hard to fix it, and things do not turn out the way I want. I ask for some guidance, and the message I receive is about valuing life. My mother is battling cancer, and I realize that no matter how pretty you look, if you are not healthy, it is pointless. I'm sure I created all the experiences that made me who I am today—that is part of my path. In the end, it's all for the better, and I begin to learn to accept that I was okay the way I am. That level of acceptance is what really helped me to get out of the roller coaster of always wanting to fix myself.

I start looking at all the other things that are good about me, like how I am always a good friend and how my friends describe me as having good, charming qualities. And I think maybe this is the way God looks at people, for what they are and not for how they look.

And that's the beginning of a new way of being, accepting that there are things I cannot change about my physical beauty and deciding to put my attention more in the *essence* of me.

It takes commitment and time to be free from self-judgment. The best thing is to acknowledge things and allow them to be what they are.

Overcoming that period of my life is one of the best experiences I've had. Now I can create differently. My worth no longer depends on how I look. While I still like to take care of myself looking put together, wearing makeup, or getting a treatment, it's not done from the space of fixing but rather from the space of enhancing, celebrating myself, playing, and having fun.

As I keep changing and growing my self-esteem, I get plenty of opportunities to go one step higher in the direction of self-acceptance and love.

I used to think that taking care of myself means looking pretty, but there's more than that; it's about honoring my needs, loving and gifting to myself, attention, care, time and having a balanced life.

I join a coaching program that helped me to grow and learn how to help others to do the same. Life is an amazing journey; all the lessons and experiences appear as we walk the path of honoring ourselves and others.

When I get into my heart, I start noticing what is important.

One day, as I am participating in a Melukat ceremony in Bali, while the healer is pouring water on my head and inviting me to purify and release what no longer serves me, I feel the beauty of my spirit in my heart. I'm there just wrapped in a sarong, with neither makeup nor fancy clothing. My hair is wet, water dripping throughout my body, and I'm still *feeling* so beautiful. My essence has emerged, and that light coming from inside me showed as a blissful glow radiating in all directions. My face is relaxed, my eyes are closed, and my smile reflects the ecstasy of what it's like to be one with everything. At that moment, I know love and peace.

In my journey, I've gone from feeling not enough to embracing life with a sense of being whole and loved.

True Power is in knowing that everything that happens can be a pathway and an opportunity to grow. For me, this power resides in my heart.

When I am in my True Power, I have been told there is a glow in me, a spark that comes from within; it is as if every cell in the body radiates with joy and love. The eyes become brighter, the posture changes, the body looks taller, and the chest expands to give room to the heart that emanates that love.

There are many things I learned along the way. They help me grow into my true beauty and essence. First, I know now how to connect with the true Source; it may be God or the universe itself. I learned that my true self shows when I'm vibrating in bliss, love, health, enthusiasm, and gratitude.

My compassion for others has grown, and that helps me be a better person. I also became more aware of my feelings and listen to them when they tell me when I'm off-center. I now feel the warmth of joy and peace because I love myself for what I truly am deep down.

In my younger years, I could only see my value based on my appearance; it's only after facing the unexpected that I realize that beauty is only a projected perception.

I continue evolving and creating, and I'm very honored to assist others in releasing their limiting patterns so they can live from their Heart and Beingness to access their True Power to live in Peace, Love, Harmony and experience Beauty.

Back to Me…
One Part at a Time

Fiorella Garibaldi

My boyfriend and I are on the balcony of his high-rise building overlooking the beautiful Miami skyline, sunny clear blue skies, people buzzing around, boats coming and going in the warmth of a spring day.

I can hear jazz music from the apartment in the background adding to the splendid day. It's a typical Sunday, and everyone seems to be having such a great time. I, on the other hand, am dying. I can't believe his words. I try to lie to myself wishing and hoping secretly that he'd choose me. I want this so bad. I want to be chosen. Please, someone, choose me!

But instead, I feel so worthless, so insignificant, so little, so betrayed. He tells me, "Yes, I am married. I never told you because we were having so much fun I didn't want to ruin it…and we have plans to live together here". They had been living in different countries so far. He kept looking at the horizon and continued, "I'm sorry. I don't think I can give you what you want."

I have never really asked for anything other than what we have, maybe I did want more, but at this point, I was just happy to have the leftover love he was able to give. My body feels so weak listening to his truth, and I crumble to the ground. The sun is shining, yet I'm covered by darkness. Every word he keeps saying feels like a stab in my heart. I have lost this battle. I'm wounded beyond anything I've ever experienced, and believe me, I've experienced rejection before, but this one is different.

The perfect day has become foggy, and the bright sunny day has been clouded by uncontrollable tears flooding my heart. I'm drowning in pain, and I can't seem to be able to come up for air. I lose track of time. I can't understand how someone I trusted and loved so much is doing this. Why? But he's not choosing me this time. He's a married man who entered my life as a single man, with a bunch of painful lies. I have never fully known his secret until this day. Even though my intuition all along knew something was very off, I haven't dared to really find out the truth.

At some point, he looks at his phone and says, "I have to go. I have a running meeting with a friend." That was it. I left. I drive back home and stop at a parking lot and continue to cry. I feel so ashamed and embarrassed, I don't want to go home because my parents are there. I don't want to tell them how stupid I have been.

The universe has tried countless times to show me the truth in so many different ways—from friends' gatherings where he would avoid to introduce me to his friends, physically running away from me the whole night to avoid questions, to him forgetting to take off his wedding ring when he came to see me, and to kindly refusing to take pictures with me as he wasn't much into pictures. It really has been there in front of my face all along, but I was not ready. I was blinded by my wounds and scared to be left alone—until today—and he was not going to give up his life for me.

What was so wrong with me? I keep hearing in my head. *Why couldn't any men see me as worthy of anything else but a good time?*

I'm a responsible, hardworking, independent woman, who likes to have fun, but everyone seems to only focus on the fun side and not see beyond that. It's so painful. I'm so tired of being used and left like a piece of crap, like I don't deserve any better.

This is more than another breakup. It's a deeper cry than this man. It's a cry of my entire reality being shattered. It's the cry of years of betraying myself. It's the pain of trusting others more than myself. It's the ache of a lifetime not being me.

As a child, I grew up feeling wrong, quiet, and shy. Speaking up was not my thing. I moved from Peru to Miami at age ten. I was immediately placed in school, and not knowing the language really impacted me. All I remember was being very confused all the time, with a kind of fog around me, kids talking to me and me not being able to answer and often being mocked for not understanding. I felt so alone and so little. As a result of my environment, I developed a survival skill of shutting down, and my expression of self was cut off. I liked being invisible and immersed myself in my drawings to escape the confusing world out there.

As an adult, I often accept less than what I deserve, even when it feels like shit. I choose alcohol and drugs to numb the pain of not liking myself; they've become my best friends as they give me the courage to push aside the shy girl and become wild, lovable, and accepted. For the first time in my life, I start to feel accepted, and people actually like me.

I spend countless nights in clubs' bathrooms drugging myself only to not remember anything the next day and waking up covered in shame not knowing what I have done the night before. I drank until I blacked out and got into relationships desperately looking for love. My life has been a whole pretend show. I have so many masks and played so many roles that I forgot who I was. Although from the outside, everything looks great and perfect—I'm the head of the wardrobe department for a big television company, I make great money, and I have bought my first apartment at age twenty-four, drive a convertible, look good, and know how to have a good time—my life inside is painful. Waking up is dreadful, work is not filling my heart anymore, and this relationship is killing me softly, and I can't bear with it anymore.

After the breakup, I bury myself in isolation for the next year, away from the world, friends, and parties. It feels like someone has died. Indeed, parts of me have died. I'm grieving the pain of loss. I sit countless evenings alone in my room, staring at nothing, feeling everything. It's something I have always tried to desperately avoid, but this time, I can't escape it. I need to *feel.* I know the only way out of my pain is through it. In those endless, silent days, I dive into the depths of every feeling and decide to pick up all the fractured parts little by little. Some are angry, some are hurt, some are ashamed, some are sad, and others are lonely and tired.

I sit on that chair curiously welcoming them one by one; every feeling is like a little baby coming back home to me. In this process, I start to learn what they really wanted, needed, and so desperately long for. I spend hours with them talking, hearing them, and being curious. I take the time, and I'm there for them like I've never been before, like a big, loving, nurturing mother would do.

Some days are easier than others. Some days, I feel like I want to die. Some parts are so hurt it takes so much compassion and forgiveness toward myself. Some days, everything is numb and seems like nothing is happening, and I'm just going back. Some days, I can see the sun coming in through the blinds of pain. But one thing is for sure, I'm not going back, so I grab every book that inspires me, read every article that speaks to me, invest my money in a coaching program, listen to every mentor that resonates with my story, and do the work as if my life depends on it—and indeed, it does.

I can't tell you exactly when it happened. It's not like one day I woke up and everything has been magically healed; it takes constantly showing up for myself, daily work, lots of love, and a lot of patience to become that one thing I so desperately look for all my life. I've become the most precious thing I have: I've become my source of love. It's me I have been looking for all along!

This understanding has been my biggest medicine. After feeling and allowing myself to bring all parts of me back home, becoming my infinite source of love has changed everything in my life. I've stopped being a victim of the world. I've stopped judging myself so harshly. I've forgiven myself for engaging in situations that did not honor my being. I've become my best friend and the one thing I love the most, in such a powerful way that the need to share this with everyone started to emerge. I can't keep all this goodness to myself, and an undeniable need to share this with everyone ready to listen is what drives my life today.

I can't tell you that I wake up every day jumping up and down in joy, no, but I've learned ways of connecting back into my source of power, through moving, breathing, feeling, plugging back to my heart, listening, and allowing. I can navigate through the heavy days in whatever way. The ultimate truth that everything is already inside of me gives me the strength and the motivation to continue with my vision of the life I know is possible.

Since that powerful "breakup" day—that's how I see it now—so many things have changed. I've quit my lifelong job in the TV industry as a costume designer, leaving the "safety" of a paycheck, and decided to become a life coach where I now make people look and feel good from the inside out. I've changed the pretty dresses for inner confidence and the latest fashion for unwavering love. I've also met an incredible man in Hawaii while in a retreat, and we've gotten married a year later in a beautiful forest ceremony.

It is the most perfect day of summer. I've managed to gather my closest friends and family in the middle of the Swedish forest. As I walk up the little hill, my dad holds me and makes jokes to release my nerves, or maybe his. As we approach the ceremonial space, I just keep thinking, *Wow, this is a dream.* It all looks like a fairy tale, better than I could've ever imagined. As we step into the circle, the flute plays in the background. I can feel the love of everyone around us.

Daniel stands in front of me as we hold hands and look into each other's eyes. Glimpses of the sun peak through the pine trees, shining on his big blue eyes. He has shown me what unconditional love and support really look like; this man has taught me that it's safe to ask for my needs, it's safe to be me, all of me, that it's okay to disagree and still love each other, and that no matter how triggered or how challenging life gets, if we keep creating the space for honest and vulnerable self-expression without judgment, we will overcome any struggles. The gong plays in the background as we say yes to love, and a strong vibrating sound ripples out into every cell of my being as if it was sealing this union and this intention on a deeper level.

We now live and work together in Sweden, facilitating people and holding retreats and workshops around the world, and he continues to support me every day in the pursuit of my dreams.

My new life in Sweden is wonderful; as I'm writing this, the seasons are changing. After a long winter filled with bon fires, long dark days, and cozy socks all day, I now get to feel the warmth of the sun and the light coming back. As I sit here on the porch, the trees are filling themselves up with life once again, and the flowers are blooming everywhere gracing us with their scent. I can hear the birds singing, and everyone seems to be rejoicing that we've made it after the long winter darkness. And just like nature teaches us, the darkness is not always a bad thing but rather the rich soil from where we get to grow.

This whole adventure called life had taught me that my true power really has always been inside of me, an inner potential that no matter where I go or where I end up, as long as I keep digging into my heart for truth and answers, I will always be okay!

Had you told me back then that out of that incredible pain, I would end up sharing my story to inspire others to love themselves and reach within for answers, I would've not believed you. But I now know that the universe is working in mysterious ways always steering us toward the highest and best for us and all.

The Power of the Breath

Sandra Ann Grant

I'm in survival mode. I've nothing more to give. All I have is a history of being not good enough, fear of failure, failed marriages, job losses, abuse, low self-esteem, victim, burnout, depression, trauma, unable to feel or express emotion, chronic fatigue…

Now I'm losing everything: love, family, home, health, money. My marriage is so toxic we are all sick and have to physically separate.

I'm spending time with my mum overseas, trying to regain my energy and self-esteem.

"Happy Easter! What have you been up to?" I ask my two young boys on the phone.

"We've been looking at houses," they say.

My mind is racing. The place they mention is a six-hour drive from where we live. "What about the caravan down there?"

"We're moving…"

What? I was hoping that they would live with me on my return. Instead, they move away with their father, ten days after I arrive back from overseas.

Change of residence, school, lifestyle.

No consultation. No agreement. No recourse.

And I have no energy to fight.

The only way I can be hurt is losing my boys. I cannot bear the thought of not having my two children, or of them being separated from each other.

I feel powerless, distraught, angry, heartbroken, betrayed, grief-stricken.

After the shock comes the flood of tears.

Eventually, I reach for help through a transformational coaching facilitation. I dial the phone number at the appointed time.

I'm alone, sitting on my bed, my back leaning against the pillow propped up against the wall, knees bent, feet flat.

My whole body is shaking. I am neither hot nor cold, yet I am shivering. Sweat is pouring from my armpits. My forehead is cool. I'm not sick.

My heart is thumping louder and faster.

"Keep breathing" I remind myself. "Take a deep breath so you can get the words out."

My focus intensifies. Ready. Waiting.

Then I say, "Hello," with as much control as I can muster. "I have been crying and coughing for weeks, releasing emotions, talking to my inner child, releasing again. There's something more…I need help."

Q: "Let's ask your little one: 'What are you afraid of, sweetheart?'"

A: "Afraid of getting into trouble and doing it wrong."

Q: "Who was it that made you feel like you were wrong? Mum or dad, or both? Is what you're feeling worse than being wrong?"

I have snatches of my thoughts: "Have no voice… my truth…knowing…"

"They were lying."

It's both a question and confirmation.

So much love, compassion, and softness flood through the questions to my little one, my inner child. She, the little me, feels safe to answer.

Q: "Feel what's coming up…Make it safe to feel. What's the worst thing that could happen?"

A: "It's like being left to die."

Q: "Which is not loved, not safe, not cared for. Do you think this is your fault?"

A: "No."

Q: "So would this have happened if you weren't here?"

A: "No."

Q: "There you go. So she *does* think it's her fault, even existing…"

I don't remember any words that are said to me other than, "Allow that…nod your head …"

A new surge of emotion comes through. My eyes are screwed up, crying uncontrollably—but there are no tears. It's like a silent scream, through my eyes. My shivering breath is barely audible. My chest is shuddering.

I try to comply, even though I can't be seen.

Choosing. Trusting. Allowing. Releasing. Letting go. Surrendering to the moment.

Letting go of what? A lifetime of feeling, at some deep level, that I should not exist, should never have existed; and the world would be better off without me.

By me existing, all this terrible stuff has happened; if I didn't exist, it wouldn't happen.

I feel deep grief because I've been denying my own life, my own self. Finally, I'm giving myself the love and safety to let it out and start living—to be excited and proud to be living and know it's not my fault.

"Yes!" I feel understood—validated.

Q: "It's like you take all the loving, feeling parts of you and hide them from yourself."

More words are said, but I don't recall them.

But then I feel peace! Everything stops.

I'm aware of my knees. It's as if they're not part of me. They are perfectly still.

My top is wet and clammy, stuck to my skin.

My breath is calm.

I observe all the parts of me in a detached way.

It's over. I'm okay.

It's all a blur.

A huge thunderstorm struck during my conversation. It has now cleared, replaced by a double rainbow.

I don't yet know the full impact or implications of this session. I know I'm still releasing the grief. I'm more aware. I reflect further on the deep revelation.

I know my life hasn't been great, but until now, I haven't realized that I didn't want to exist. If *I* am hiding parts of myself, it's no wonder I don't feel seen, heard, recognized, valued, or loved by others.

Thinking that *I* am responsible, it's no wonder I try to be Superwoman, working so long and hard and putting everyone else's needs ahead of mine.

And being "my fault" for bad stuff happening gives some insight as to why I didn't even realize I was being abused.

It seems that I could never be successful, or recognized as such, because deep down, I don't believe I deserve it—that I'm worthy of it or good enough.

I see myself as a victim rather than a powerful person. I'm always afraid of conflict, fearful of threats.

And now that my boys no longer live with me, I have no real purpose or motivation. There is no joy.

If I'm not somebody's wife, mother, teacher, etc., who am I?

Why am I here? What's the point?

What do I want to do?

I have more questions than answers.

All attempts to get a vision of my future lead to more deep crying.

If my soul has a vision, my mind can't yet put it into words.

I'm not motivated by anything on the material plane.

I want to be "happy" and complete my life purpose/soul contract—whatever I came here to do.

I really don't have a definitive answer, but more of an "open to infinite possibilities" invitation.

I wonder how I can make the biggest impact on the world, with the least amount of effort, whilst having the most fun, for the highest good of all.

I resolve to change everything in my "old" life and start again, looking for "something"—I'm not sure what—that will make a difference to my life and the lives of others.

Fast-forward.

I enjoy spending quality time with my two amazing sons who are making a difference in their own unique ways. Our connection through love remains even when we are physically apart.

Being open to "infinite possibilities" and following my intuitive guidance have finally led me here. It's not something I had ever imagined would happen.

I'm about to speak on stage in Sedona, Arizona. The outside temperature is close to 120 degrees Fahrenheit (48.9 degrees Celsius). It's significantly cooler inside the theatre. Backstage, as I make final preparations, I start to tremble violently all over. I can't stop.

How am I going to be able to walk on stage, let alone speak? For twenty minutes, I try and shake off the energy that is shooting through me like a high-voltage current.

I deliberately shake my arms, hands, legs, trying to release the energy, telling myself, "Breathe…calm down. What am I going to say?"

Time to go to the stage wing and get mic'd up. I'm grateful there is someone there to show me the way through the labyrinth. It's all a blur to me. Someone else is attaching the microphone.

My mind is alternating between mentally asking for all the help I can, trying to control my shaking, focusing on breathing, and telling myself what I have to do: walk to the *X* on stage, smile as you look at the audience, and say, "My name is Sandy Grant."

The announcer is saying something—a series of things. I'm not sure if I'm supposed to be going on yet or not. Waiting, waiting. All my senses are on full alert.

I'm walking on stage. The lights are glaring. *So* bright. I can't see anyone or anything. But I look and smile at the audience as if I can.

Still shivering on the inside, I take a long, slow, deep breath, and begin to speak. Then I take in another deep breath, followed by a *very long* pause, as I try to manage my emotions, my voice, and wait for the next download of words to come into my head.

Many deep intakes of breath. Many long pauses. At times, my voice quivers. After another deep breath, I ask: "Why are you here? Not just now, but why are you here, on the planet? What are you here to bring? And what's stopping you from bringing it?"

As I speak of my journey, and my experiences in life, I'm occasionally aware of the audience— intakes of breath, whispered comments, laughter, and brief spontaneous applause.

I continue: "So my message to you is keep going, even if you feel like you're not important, that you don't have the qualifications. You have life experience. You've been through it."

"There is no need for you to block out the pain. You can hand it over. You can ask that the people that you've been helping can still be served without it having to be through you—that it can come from an infinite source."

"The message to you is that you are important. You have a special mission in this world, and it doesn't matter if you don't know what it is. And it doesn't matter if you don't know how you're going to do it." While I'm talking, I feel like it's a different voice— Source—speaking through me. "Just know that you are important. You are needed. You are special. You are loved. And by being that, by being that beacon of love and light, you're going to have an impact on the people around you."

"Thank you very much for being here."

Loud applause. Relief. I still feel the tension in my body, but I'm aware that I'm smiling– fully.

An open session follows for questions or comments from the audience. I need to shade my eyes with my hand to see beyond the glaring lights to who's speaking.

I'm surprised at the impact I have made. There's a woman in tears and a guy who "can relate" to my story "even though the details are different." Someone else comments that they "feel the love" coming through me.

As I leave the stage, there is a *big* sense of relief, of letting go of my story, and of being seen, heard, acknowledged, and making a difference.

As a celebration gift to myself I buy a beautiful, unique, multifaceted "magic" Opalite pendant that flashes different colors—blue, orange, purple, green. In direct sun, it reflects turquoise "disco light" spots.

I wear it always; it is a constant reminder to myself that I'm a unique shining light in this world. I give myself permission to shine.

This is my portal into infinite possibilities.

*

My true power is twofold:

First, I have my connection to a higher power—an infinite source of love, guidance, and support. Call it

Source, Spirit, or Universe (some may call it God; I am spiritual, but not religious).

I know that I'm a reflection of this higher power. I allow myself to be a channel of Divine love and light.

I connect to this higher power daily, through thought, meditation, and daily writing; it empowers me to access guidance and messages through my intuition/higher self.

At times, there are connections to loved ones who have passed, "past life" insights, general insights, reassurances, things to focus on, understanding, and "aha!" moments.

In my darkest/most fearful or uncertain times, this is my inspiration—this higher power.

The second one is self-love. I have learned to be all of me—to love and unconditionally accept *all* of me.

I started by looking at my face in the mirror and saying, "I love you." Now I look at my whole naked body and say, "I love you."

When I have love for myself, nothing else matters—I always have love. When I stop judging myself and others, I stop being judged.

I have also stopped "adding story" to what others say or do and stopped making things personal/about me.

As a result, I no longer have drama in my life. I live in the moment. I accept things that are outside of my control. I have become more aware of thoughts, feelings, emotions, even pain, that are not mine. And I let it go.

I live in a state of abundance and joy. I'm free. I trust that I'm loved and supported—within myself. I trust in Source.

For me, standing in "your true power" means standing for myself, in love; being my true/authentic self; acknowledging and accepting where I have been; standing without judgment; recognizing the transformation I have undergone, through facing and releasing fear, anger, grief, pain and other emotions; and choosing my reality from an infinite menu of possibilities.

The more awareness I have, the more I can choose my reality. I notice my thoughts, feelings, beliefs, and ask myself, "Did I consciously choose this, or is it an automatic response or awareness of something in the collective consciousness—the global soup of other people's stuff?"

When I consciously choose from an infinite menu of possibilities, I consider, "What's the highest expression at this moment?" (For example, love, joy, gratitude, or abundance).

In this way, I am able to choose my focus, not just react to what shows up, and create my reality, regardless of what is going on for others.

The Lightness of Being

Dionnie Simone

The view from up here is beautiful. I feel high above the real world. The freshly cut grass below is a reflective green yellow, and the driveway pebbles shine a bright white. The climbing tree on my front lawn is my closest confidant. The sun warms my face through the sparse leaves, and the well-proportioned branches are perfectly positioned for my reach. Since I was a child, this has always been my favorite place to escape, think, reflect, and connect.

Now at seventeen years old, I seek the safety of the canopy once more. What great news to receive a letter of offer from The Royal Ballet School, Covent Garden, England! The feeder school to the Royal Ballet Company. An opportunity to attend the prestigious ballet school. A dream come true for an aspiring ballet student like me.

But like always, when I dare to dream, something or someone comes in and takes my choice away. I know Dad is concerned about my safety and me being so far away from Australia, but this is a huge deal for me.

Classical ballet is both rewarding and challenging. Dance is a freedom where my soul connects to my body and brings so much joyful expression.

To me, the cotton wool wrapping to protect a child feels more like a choking corset or a cage. I cannot argue or stick up for myself as this decision entirely lies in Dad and Mum's hands.

The tree offers no solace or advice today.

Over the years, I slowly become less sure of myself, less independent, and I feel like no one is on my side. This pattern of asking for something and being told "no" and finally not choosing anything has followed me into adulthood. I've married a strong-minded individual, and I feel I cannot express myself or continue dancing—as it's not an acceptable profession.

I've forgotten my power and become a victim of circumstances. A victim of others and easy prey because that's the vibration I exude. I'm learning to replace my desires with the desires of others, even willing to sacrifice my opinion and intuition for another's stronger reasoning skills. It's easier to play this part. I don't have to try as hard, and I can live my life through their hard work and success. I'm compromising my wishes so much that I'm *barely* myself anymore. That has become my personality. I've played the part for so long and so well that it has become me.

I'm sure I have free will and that I'm choosing, but that is not so. If you appear more assured than me, then I'll give my power to you. If you're confident, loud, bold, scary, or knowledgeable, then I'll retreat, salute you, and adopt your views as mine. I'll give my power away to the external and please, worship, and follow you. If it gets too hard, I'll stop asking for what I want and ask instead what you want.

I'm a queen who has lost her crown. I'm locked in a cage without a key. To the outside world, it looks grand. I have jewels. I shop till I drop—cars, houses, a king, a prince, and princesses. I attend every ball. This dream existence sold to me all my life. Why am I not happy? I'm depressed, fearful, uncreative, and unfulfilled. The overriding sentiment each day is of doom and gloom.

I went to a place so dark and full of despair.
There wasn't a breeze
nor oxygen
Nothing green grew there.
It was a place to wallow, sit, and sink still lower.
Hold your breath,
Be compressed.
Heart beating, blood donor.
The shadows attacked from all sides.
The black crow descended.
Insides clenched, chest constricted,
Joy ended.
The light was far away, only a glimmer,
But never gone.
I swallowed my pride but choked on it halfway down.
Pride lies in limbo with the tears fighting a battle of their own.
The scars rose to the surface.
Time heals, they say.
The hardened crust picked, hurts fresh now as the first day.
Not a pretty place.

There's always a turning point. It can be at the highest of highs, visiting beautiful sceneries, traveling to wonderful places and having incredible experiences, or it can be at the opposite end of the spectrum, feeling extremely low, depressed, anxious, and stressed, when you're being all the worst facets of the human condition. Now that I've arrived here, I'm separated from the self—my worst conglomeration of fears. I'm not conscious. All my behaviors are automatic responses from my past, programmed in so well that they take over me. My body chemistry is programmed also to be depressed, negative, and lost.

How can I be so fortunate yet remain so miserable? I'm therefore ungrateful, unworthy, undeserving. "Just be happy! What's wrong with me?" I beat myself up over this dilemma as I attempt to solve it. I'm far from my true spirit, and I exist in a trance. I live in regret and no longer dream of a bright future. I've no choices. It's fruitless even trying. I'm separate from life, and this damn pre- and postnatal depression is spiraling me down further. I feel like I have dementia. Where's my mind's clarity? Chest infection after chest infection, trouble breathing, suffocating, suspected asthma. Test after test. No, it's not asthma. Fear and grief have infected my body, affecting my lungs. I'm being crushed. Gasping and burdened, I see I'm completely caged in and suffocated. This manifestation in the physical body seems like the final straw. I feel weak and forgotten.

I feel that life is passing me by, and I'm not there to see it. I'm not present. I'm absent in my own life's creation. The grey cloud is descending. Everything I look at is dull.

I'm falling, failing, squashed, a blank stare.
Ripping, tearing sadness,
Emotional well, pull out my hair.
Barrier, blockade, one path only,
My highway, gloom.
Sinking weight, heavy chest,
High wall, dark cloud. Boom!
Rushed, trapped, teary poison,
Shutdown system, spitting words.
Judgment, tight, weakened, shaken,
Prickled, thorn, torn, stirred.
Beating water, short-winded.
No fresh air. So tight.
Pulled, tattered, bitten, stung,
Chopped, pushed, without flight.
Disconnected, maneuvered, fed up,
Stretched, split, bound and tied.
Shaky, crumpled, lost my footing,
Shattered, heart cavity open wide.
Flattened, mistaken, ruled,
Silent scream, ashamed, succumbed.
Empty, shriveled, closed shut,
Lost,
Numb.
What have I become?

I'm so disconnected from life at this point that I'm willing to take a life—my own. I sneak like a burglar out my back sliding door. The winter air is chilled, but

I feel nothing. I don't need to conceal my exit as no one misses me. Dinner is well and truly over, and the kitchen is tidy, but the light is still on. The children are asleep in bed, and my husband hasn't noticed. My focus now is the water and the escape. The garden and tennis court have both disappeared from sight. Tunnel vision in every respect. There's no way out of the pain and segregation I feel from life except to force a different outcome by way of the death of my troubled soul. I don't care about hurting others because I'm hurting so badly. I don't care for my well-being because I am in such unease and maybe this will allow me to feel free.

I jump loudly into the dark pool, secretly hoping that it will alert someone—anyone. Dying by drowning is a very peaceful way to die, I was once told. As I let the air fully expel and feel my lungs burn underwater, a glowing white light appears in front of me. It's accompanied by a low voice, saying, "Now is not the time. You can't leave. You're not ready to die. You are destined for greatness!"

The voice is very familiar. It's my own—sent from beyond space and time, from a future me at a retreat. My suffering, desperate self hears the message and fully comprehends instantly. I move up to the surface and revel in the night air. I rise and walk out of the pool like someone who has just received the best news of their life. My head held high, I imagine a long robe trailing me as I walk. Shivering and wet through, I make my way still unnoticed, to the shower.

My Spirit calls out to me in desperation to make changes. I'm sorry I've been closed. I'm sorry I stopped trusting and listening to you. I begin to wake up and move cautiously out of the coma. I keep watch on where I'm powerless. I notice I'm giving my power away. I'm not choosing for my greater good. I'm running on default. It's overriding my joy and light. Playing small has never been me—but it has become me over time. From experience, I learned that if I stand out, I'm ridiculed, and I've nothing to offer anyway. But something *has* to change. I must *do* something different.

A sign grabs my attention during a family walk: "Beach Yoga." Yes, I will choose this time for myself. I've never done yoga before, but being an ex-dancer is a comforting thought.

At 9:30 a.m., I'm on the mat complete with headphones for a silent yoga practice. A man sweeps his metal detector over the nearby beachfront sand, and the instructor says to us over the headphones, "He doesn't realize that what he's looking for is on the inside, and he won't find it there." I feel the sun on my bare arms and face and commence turning my attention inward. My muscles remember how to glide me through movements, and though tighter than before, they adjust with ease to the flow. I smile as I recognize my abilities.

Day 1: I notice my body on the mat, and I breathe effectively.

Day 2: I feel more connected with my body, and my body thanks me for devoting time to stretch, balance, and connect.

Day 3: I'm fully reunited with my body, my mind has quietened, and I enjoy focusing solely on myself.

The walk back home is surreal and ultimately life-changing, as I'm about to find out. I tread along the grass just above the high-water line of the front beach. I feel the effects of yoga off the mat. I'm present, my mind has stopped its relentless negative dialogue, and I notice the waves—gentle, rhythmic—lapping repeatedly at the shore. My heart is soaring.

I look ahead and see the grey cloud I've been living in. It looms over like a foreboding, thick, velvet stage curtain. The same grey cloud fogs my mind and memory. This exact grey cloud makes me think I'm aging rapidly and puts my forgetfulness down to dementia. But I'm too young! I approach the sand and feel every grain on my bare feet. This cloudy apparition drives home the awareness that I've lost the color and vibrancy of my world, my vitality, and all sense of joy and happiness. I'm shocked to find myself face-to-face with this smog.

As I walk toward it, it begins rising. Yippee! I clap as I know a more joyous play is about to unfold. Slowly, it lifts to reveal the brightest, most blinding hues I've ever seen. This slow Technicolor unwrapping is tantalizing and awe-inspiring. All I can do is stare, transfixed by the intensity, fearlessness, and conviction of nature to reveal itself to me in this way. Gratitude, peace, personal power, clarity, conviction, conciliation, and a will to survive all strike me at once. The urge to not only survive but also to thrive, relocate, live my dreams settles into my awareness and body. I know I will never doubt my abilities again.

Now the fog is gone, my perceived dementia symptoms likewise. I can recall what I had for breakfast yesterday. I know what I wore a few days ago and remember what I've to do later. I've been reset. All my faculties back online. I'm alive. The connection to Source and to all is evident and strong. It's often more than what the physical body can stand due to its high vibrational nature, and I know I will continually elevate my frequency to access even more. Many spiritual encounters such as this regularly show up, but this is a turning point.

If this profound encounter could happen after three days of yoga, then I wonder what could happen if I do it daily. I know I'll teach it and share the benefits with everyone.

Now it gets even more exciting. I notice my behaviors, guard my thoughts, and have an unquenchable thirst for knowledge. My teachers show up, and to them I feel so much gratitude. Honesty and inspiration are a must when working with someone to better yourself, and it enables you to quickly move through the garbage and move toward your best self and life. I devour books and attend seminars and courses.

Staying present and noticing my programming requires both focus and vigilance. By day 3 of a conference, I'm really paying attention and remaining in joy. I find myself so happy, free without a care, making choices, then instantly manifesting. With my intuition extremely heightened, I feel connected to all things, and as such, I feel powerful like I have a magnificent presence.

I'm having the most amazing experiences, and I'm effortlessly in the flow. Instead of looking outside of myself for inspiration, I'm my own superhero. I see what's possible for all of us when we reunite with the Source and remember the gifts we possess. The world looks very different. This vision has all animals living in harmony, dazzling inventions, and the purity of nature evident and noticed by all.

Best of all is the feeling we have when we tap into our true power for everyone's greater good. I adore seeing the beauty and talents that exist in people even if they're oblivious to it. I enjoy reminding others to look inside for what they've hidden and forgotten about themselves so they can open to more also.

My daughter witnesses me quiet babies, conjure songs, and have things just show up like offerings of tea and water whenever I ask for it. She says, 'Mum, you are magic!"

I reply, "Yes, I am, but so are you." I begin to explain that she's capable of this but needs to mind her state of Being. I teach her every night at bedtime about her infinite self, capabilities, and choices. She discovers some of her gifts, and her being open to receiving without judgment allows her access to new outcomes. I see her alter her internal dialogue around going to bed, and a once-anxious event emerges as a chance to consciously plan, feel good, and learn more of her power.

Giving myself back my power has been the greatest gift of my journey. My power is choosing consciously and understanding I'm part of the Divine creation, and therefore, I'm infinitely abundant and supported. I'm a creator, and my life is only limited by the limitations I place on myself. I live from this place of knowing; therefore, I cannot let others choose for me. I won't sell myself short again, and I cannot live by default. I will give it a go even if you tell me no. I will persevere with passion, and I no longer have the nagging psychopathic voice in my head chastising me. I will never feel held back, caged, and stifled. All this power exists within me!

I'm present and experiencing more of the spiritual world. The physical is created from the spiritual, so it makes sense to create from that limitless space, and then it has to show up here. Because life is a reflection of one's patterns, it's easy to keep check on how well I'm faring. All I have to do is look around.

If I'm not abundant in every respect, then there are still limitations at work. How are personal relationships? Am I happy? Am I doing what I love? Do I feel fulfilled? What's my relationship with money?

I'm no longer everything I fear, believe, tell myself, and get told. I'm not a powerless victim. I'm living life by design. As a spiritual being having a human experience, what could be better than playing in density? How clever are we to have co-created mass with form! This awareness alone makes everyone and everything you come into contact with a true miracle. The world is your stage, and the earth is a magical wonderland filled to the brim with possibilities, just waiting for you to act on it.

Of course, this makes life simultaneously fascinating, joyous, and challenging in each moment. With my true power, I've been able to harness my true purpose to remember and journey back to myself. To remember my Divine nature and express it to the world in my unique, creative way, harnessing the trials of my upbringing, experiences along the way, and my gifts. To be my complete self and spread my joy. As I ascend the levels of awakening, I vibrate higher and am privy to more knowledge. Now I embody those lessons of life, become the knowledge, and teach it to others. Looking at everything through the eyes of love for the self allows true connection and life takes on new meaning.

Today, I have the privilege of guiding others through yoga classes where I share my palpable love for this practice. Many students have unexpected visions and feelings of being nurtured in love during my sessions. I also help transform lives through my empowering meditations and coaching sessions. I've taken yoga and meditation to an online platform to reach more people. There's no greater joy than to watch others become their best self.

Beautiful Life Equation

Barbara Harumi Otis

I think I'm adding more to my life. I appear to have a perfect life. I have a husband who makes a good living, two wonderful boys, a nice house, and savings and investments for retirement. Yet I'm still searching for something. I'm constantly taking many different healing modality classes and workshops as well as reading many self-help and new-thought books. I'm reaching for more: I long for more love and joy in my life. I join the Life Transformed Coaching Program to have a life that I love and earn money while being myself and doing what I enjoy. My equation is this: beautiful life + more love & joy = bliss. It seems so simple, like 1 + 1 = 2.

But then my husband wants to have a conversation with me. He tells me that we are getting a divorce. I am devastated. This should not be a surprise. All the signs have been right there. He has been mad and yelling at the boys and me for the six months prior to this conversation. Five years earlier, he told me he wanted a divorce. At that time, I asked him, "What if I don't want a divorce?"

At that time, I knew that neither of us was happy nor did we know how to get there, but I'm not sure if we can save our marriage. He is absolutely sure he wants a divorce, but then a month later, he's absolutely sure he does not want one. I cannot understand how quickly he can change his mind about such a complex decision, which involves both of us and will also affect our boys. There are never any discussions; he simply informs me after he decides.

He's always so quick and sure of his decisions. I have a hard time making decisions or choices. I have always been more aware of what others want for me or from me than what it is that I want. I remember when I was younger, my mom wanted me to become an accountant. That never sounded like something I wanted to do. She kept suggesting, and I kept getting irritated until we fought about it.

When I told her, "That is not what I want to do with my life!" she asked me, "What do you want to do?" I had no idea. I had spent my energy on knowing and resisting what she wanted. I had never stopped to ask myself what I wanted; I only knew what I didn't want.

It takes me a long time to trust my husband again. For three years, I live in a tense and anxious state. I think he might change his mind again at any moment. Four years later, I eventually trust that we are going to stay together and make things work. I'm finally fully opening my heart again and looking forward to living our lives together. I start to plan a trip to Tahiti for our twenty-fifth wedding anniversary (which would have been the following year).

But now he's adamant about getting his divorce. I feel like the rug is being pulled out from under me, and my world is falling apart. Instead of that trip to Tahiti to celebrate twenty-five years of marriage, we are having meetings with mediators and eventually lawyers on our way toward a divorce. It's real now. My marriage is not dying anymore—it's dead. My heart is broken. It has been wounded and protected by stronger and more fortified walls before, but this time, all of that has broken down completely. I'm so scared and vulnerable. I cry every single day.

All these years of marriage thrown away so easily. Have I completely wasted my life? Was anything I believed ever true? As my world swirls in confusion and doubt, I have only one thing I can hold onto: I have two great children that have come out of this marriage. If nothing else, that has to be enough. Although they don't say much, when I am filled with doubt, they reassure me that this is what's best for everyone in the family.

There are so many horrible critical voices that keep repeating hateful thoughts over and over in my head: "You are a failure." "You can't do anything right." "You have been tossed aside and dismissed." "You are worthless." "He is better off without you." "No one will ever love you." "He fell in love with you when you were young and beautiful with a toned body. Who would want you now that you are old and out of shape? You wasted your youth and beauty." "You wasted your life." "You do not have a career or know how to do anything." "You have no value." "How will you survive? You are going to die." "You may as well die. You have no reason to live."

I know these are irrational and not true, yet I feel them deeply. I have a lot of work to do. Some of which I can do by myself with the many tools and techniques I have learned. But I also rely heavily on trusted teachers, mentors, and a few fellow coaches. Every day I recite the Ganesh mantra, tap with EFT, and I repeat the Hawaiian practice of forgiveness and reconciliation over and over many thousands of times when my mind is racing with unhelpful thoughts.

It is very awkward living together while trying to come to an agreement through mediation. It's my soon-to-be-ex-husband's birthday. What do we do? We decide to take him out to dinner. The dinner seems fine, but it apparently is not because he yells at all of us when we get back home. Lesson learned; we are definitely not doing any family type things together anymore.

It is also uncomfortable for me to see and know how eager he is to move on to another relationship. I get to see him happily texting away with another woman and sometimes going to another room to talk. I feel like I have never meant anything to him at all. "I am sorry. Please forgive me. Thank you. I love you." I repeat this phrase sometimes aloud, most of the time silently. I direct those statements to myself, to my soon-to-be-ex-husband, to our marriage, and to our divorce. Many times, it is the only thing I can do when those critical gremlin voices overtake me.

We rearrange the room situation so that we each have a bedroom, which is extremely helpful for our emotional health. The boys and I are able to retreat to our separate rooms once my soon-to-be-ex returns from work.

Now my birthday is coming up. What shall we do? I know we are not going to go to dinner as a family. I do not feel much like celebrating. Luckily, this year, my birthday falls on a Tuesday, the day I attend hula. I think that will be a fun way to celebrate my fiftieth birthday. On that day, I drive the forty minutes to hula, but when I get there, no one else is there. My teacher is sick, and I was not on the group text cancelling class because they thought I had already left for my upcoming trip. It's another blow for me. I hurry home so I can hide in my bedroom before the soon-to-be-ex gets home so he won't see me crying and how disappointed I am.

Soon I travel to Bali for my second time. This trip is unlike the one before. I have an excruciating headache and am nauseous almost the entire two and a half weeks there. We meet with many powerful traditional Balinese healers and spiritual leaders. Many times during this trip while I am receiving blessings, my head feels like it is going to explode. They encourage me to release the past and old thoughts. I tell them that I'm trying and that I do not know how. I truly would if I only knew how. I would do anything to get relief from this pain. Here I am in this exquisitely beautiful country communing, and being in ceremony, with nature but barely able to enjoy any of it. At one point, they need to carry me out. Everyone is so wonderful to me. I feel so embarrassed. I also miss out on some wonderful opportunities due to my physical distress.

I spend many hours sitting at the airport while waiting for my flight home. From time to time, I see a young couple in love, and I cry thinking of how we had been so filled with love and hope of the life we were building together. Then I see an older couple, and that reminds me we would never grow old together and of the future grandchildren we would not watch or play with together; then I cry some more. I'm mourning the promise of the life I thought I had and the one that is not to be. I'm bawling most of the six hours at the airport.

I have so many thoughts, beliefs, and expectations to unravel, feel, and release. Throughout that year and into the next, it's a daily task. As time goes by, I wake up fine. I do my morning meditations and feel very centered and peaceful. But inevitably, somewhere along my day, some small thing brings it all back. Someone might say something my ex would say, or maybe I hear a song he likes, or something in a book or movie reminds me. Then those critical gremlins all pile on me, and I am down for the count again. Okay, I will try again tomorrow.

A year later, after a full year of feeling and releasing with so many earth angels, how can I still be reduced to tears at a moment's notice? Sometimes it feels like I have made little progress. I notice that my emotional highs are higher, but somehow, that makes my lows feel even lower. I have healed so much. I have worked through every critical gremlin thought many times each, such as victimization, and expectations. I begin building my value, self-worth, and self-confidence. Those gremlins somehow howl even louder now.

Why is this still happening? As I sit wondering what else I'm still holding onto that needs to be felt and released, it suddenly becomes crystal clear. I realize that instead of standing strong in myself, I have been compromising myself by putting my focus on others. It's very subtle, but I would censor, alter, or stop myself in order to be more acceptable to others (my idea of what they want, or to be a "good girl," or a "good mother," etc.). I see that when I focus my energy on what others want or expect me to do, then I do not focus on what it is that I want. I have been doing this since before I can remember, so it's hard for me to see. I thought I did this a little, but now I can see how much I do this and how much it has cost me. I can see that instead of making anybody happier, everybody is actually unhappy and frustrated.

Underneath all the hurt and fear I have processed, I am so upset and sad for what I have given up of myself. Even with all the places I've given myself away in order to get some acceptance, love, or approval, it hasn't worked, and it would never be enough. I realize that this diluted false self will never work. Even if everyone loves and accepts me acting this way, they would be loving the cardboard version I've been creating and holding up in front of me. They would not know the true me, so I would still not feel truly loved.

Once my eyes are opened, I'm amazed at how much I've been looking for outside of myself. Deep down I felt others were more important, and that what they thought or felt mattered more than I did. I have been looking all my life for answers and reassurance from books, classes, teachers, and relationships. They can be great guides and helpers when we have lost our way, but ultimately, we each will only find our wisdom from within.

The wounded part of me would look outside to find references and cues from others. That part of me thought that was how I could stay safe. Now that I know I am safe, it is safe to be and express myself. My references and cues can only come from within myself. The wounded part felt that I was inherently wrong, what I said and did was wrong, and that it caused pain to those around me. And that if only I could say or do the right things, then everyone would be happy. Now I know that what I think, do, or say is inherently right for me and has nothing to do with how others around me are feeling. I know that the love that I have been looking for can only be found within myself.

My true power is knowing that I am loved and supported, and that my unique expression is important. Each and every one of us is loved and supported, and our unique expression is needed in this world. My life was pretty great before—now it is even better. I feel more confident, capable, and stronger. I am more relaxed and comfortable being and expressing myself around others. I am happier and have more fun and play in my life. I am intent on creating the life of my dreams.

Since I am now fully committed to choosing for me, I tune into myself each day and feel into what I want and need as well as what is fun for me. I allow myself to acknowledge that I am making this choice for me and fully receive my choice. Most of them are small simple choices: feeling the sunlight on my skin, savoring the fragrance and beauty of a flower, or enjoying the fun of dancing.

Sometimes they are bigger or more extravagant choices: I float in a sensory-deprivation tank; it is womblike but with no sound. I completely relax each of my muscles and let go of all thoughts. I surrender to the experience and feel total bliss! I allow myself to fully feel the salt water and all of life loving and supporting me.

Next we are taking off in a small plane in preparation for a tandem skydive. I think of everything that I want to let go, as well as what I am claiming in my life. As we reach high altitude, I look out the window to see the houses below that appear so small and far away. It is time to jump. This is a visceral symbol of completely letting go of everything in my life which no longer serves me and my commitment to the energies that I now invite and call forth into my life. Out we go!

What an amazing panoramic view! I have fun looking all around enjoying the view and trying to see if I can recognize anything from this new vantage point. I feel totally held and supported by the air. I am completely peaceful. I feel love, trust, and infinite possibilities!

It is important for me to tune in and choose because it's my job to take care of me. I am the one to attend to my needs—and to love, support, and celebrate myself. It seems so simple that what was missing in my equation was me; of course, I need to be included to create my beautiful life. Now my equation: myself + what brings me even more love and joy = beautiful life.

My Days Are Now Mine

Dawn Gomez

In 2015, my business was outgrowing its walls. Garden of Life Massage & Yoga Center had a waiting list several days a week with most classes at or exceeding capacity. This vision for this space had sparked fifteen years earlier, and I poured so much work into it over the past twelve years. For the first time, my efforts were finally beginning to bear fruits of a personal income that did not reflect working for minimum wage.

However, the business was not supported by its lease agreement. The landlord was not receptive to our agreement despite having a noncompete agreement. When I moved in nine years earlier, there was an error on the already signed lease regarding the pricing of signage in black and white. I could have stood my ground and not have paid the difference in the landlord's mistake. But I didn't—I agreed to make monthly payments over the next year and asked to receive the same consideration if and when the time came. I did that a lot. I gave in to peoples' needs, and when needed, my needs were not met with consideration. Truth is, I did this to myself.

We shared a wall with a franchised circuit training workout facility for women in a strip mall. As trends changed, so did how they operate. They began offering group fitness classes that morphed into offering yoga and Pilates, selling essential oils and salt lamps in their window, and then one day, I saw someone walking in with a massage table. I know there's more than enough to go around, but when I approached the landlord and the other tenant, it confirmed how little a signed agreement or someone's word is worth. I wanted us all to be successful, but I was met with resistance in our meeting. I was not feeling heard and made to think I was delusional.

(Insert Susan Powter's "Stop the Insanity!")

An excellent opportunity presented itself just across the street. It was a big opportunity—meaning a much bigger nut to crack with twice the amount of space and expand on my dream. I had a vision, a plan, and thought I had a loving partner, who also provided the same type of bodywork. I could share my clients and maintain the business-building practices I had been so good at in the past twelve-plus years, and he could create new classes to utilize his talents and abilities and benefit our community.

I dreamt of new products, like an infrared sauna and a float tank to attract a new market of clients, who may not have ever wanted massage or yoga before, and expand on what we already offered our community. I believed I had support in work and in our relationship to make this a reality. My will was strong despite the inability to obtain a business loan. I would march forward with my personal savings and build out this beautiful peaceful, free-standing space!

Close to the completion of the renovation, I learned that a home equity line I had with my former husband had come to term, and the monthly payment was now a few thousand instead of a few hundred per month. I did not know what to do. The bank had already refused me. I had almost exhausted my personal nest egg. Upon divorcing in 2012, I was unable to obtain a mortgage at that time due to the debt-to-income ratio. This deficit ratio was greatly due to my desire to give more to my business and less to myself. Truth is, I let myself slip between the cracks. I did not have my own back, but my former spouse and forever friend did.

The spring grand opening was a huge success. Everyone in the community loved this new light-filled sanctuary winding just off the main road into its park-like setting, which invites relaxation before you had even walked through our door. The yoga room had floor-to-ceiling windows with sprawling nature just beyond the glass. Every sense was thoughtfully touched with décor, lighting, and sound in the treatment rooms before a massage therapist even laid a hand on the client's body. Adding the float tank and sauna was like having a new baby in the room. Everyone wanted to see it and hold it at least once. There was such a buzz.

Unfortunately, my buzz never ceased and included never-ending berating of things no one else knew about. I was mentally carrying the burden of the worst-case scenario—self-loathing, judgment, and shame. Would I lose my home? If so, I've already used my savings, and I do not pay myself enough to provide for my needs. What would people say? They'd see I don't know anything. I am a failure.

I was exhausted and needed more than a day or two off. I had a lot of skin in the game, and my needs did not feel met by my partner romantically and domestically, not even at work. I was grateful for the support I received from my former spouse. He had obtained a mortgage for what was once our home together. I was grateful for him, but more shameful of myself since I had broken our vow.

I was riding a roller coaster of emotions. I loved what I had created. I hated what I had accepted as that I had solely destroyed. The burden of responsibility was at an all-time high. I felt everyone wanted something from me. Clients would walk right past well-informed staff members to seek answers from me. I'd walk out of a session frequently to what felt like a sucker punch of questions and requests for more.

My reserve was dried out. I needed the restoration I gave to everyone else. Nothing was left for me. I'd emotionally vomit on staff and had requested more from my partner. What I got one afternoon at work was news that he had moved out. He would continue to work at the center, but the level of communication and cooperation was at an all-time low. I was now seeing more clients than ever based on lack of commitment and attempting to grow the business just to meet the new rent with all the self-inflicted judgments placed on myself.

The fourth quarter was always busiest: seeing clients, teaching yoga, buying for our retail boutique, selling gift certificates, attending networking events and markets to attract new business, and collapsing Christmas Eve just to return the day after Christmas for business as usual on steroids, and—let's not forget— reopening on January 2 with no trace of Christmas in sight. But I did that before New Year's because I loved a fresh start for myself and all to enjoy before the new year.

I was exhausted, yet I wanted to attend the year-end class and be a part of the community for which I had worked so hard day and night. I realized I had asked a lot of myself that morning by coming to class and spent much of the class in child's pose as a prayer of surrender. I felt the earth beneath me supporting me, receiving each exhalation.

As the class ended in unison of "Om," I was quickly rattled back into the room as my neighbor turned to my eyes just blinking open and asked how my Qigong classes were going. I shuttered and recalled requesting not to talk shop today. She apparently was not happy with my request. Suddenly, every projected judgment I ever had flooded me. I had believed that if I farted on an airplane, every passenger heard it, smelled it, judged it, and knew it was me in seat 27A. If they did not, it was announced on the intercom so everyone could know and judge me.

Her reaction was that of hearing and believing every story of me being angry and aggressive by my former partner and anyone who was not happy with my actions, including myself. All I wanted was to be given the space to surrender and belong, but now I was ashamed believing that every yoga student in this packed class believed I was a horrible person and a phony. Why was there so much guilt and shame with this woman? This was the woman whom I was grateful for giving shelter to the man who was once my partner when he needed a place to go once he decided he no longer wanted to live with me. The man who no longer worked with me. The reason why I was now also teaching Qigong and attempting to regain the center's clients. Rather than accept my needs, I buckled to her judgment and packed that into the overfilled sack I was carrying right into 2017.

Fortunately, during the height of the holiday work frenzy, I signed up for a retreat, Discovering Divine Spark Within, in late January. I was so excited. I would be returning to Costa Rica many years after I had first been there and had always said I'd return.

As I was placing my suitcase in the trunk at 3:30 a.m. for the first flight out, my phone slipped from my hand and fell to the ground—shattered and nonresponsive. All the trip details were inside the broken device. If I was going to make this retreat thing happen, I had to let go of everything and trust what I have within me. I trusted I had enough information within me and enough adventure in my soul to reach my final destination:

Obtain a boarding pass from the ticket counter in Newark.

Arrive in San Jose, then locate and buy a connecting flight to Tambor.

Catch a cab off that tiny outdoor landing strip with no services to Santa Teresa, and locate my friends at the Funky Monkey Lodge. Success!

Now one check-in back to NJ to let them know I've arrived but would be completely off the radar and unplugged for the week.

It was my turn to receive. I was here to release my fears and judgments like the howler monkeys in the early hours of morning in the jungle.

We arose daily before sunrise to meditate on a covered platform in the jungle. Up until now, I had kept fear, shame, anxiety, and "not good enough" stuffed in boxes deep in my mind. I was unable and unwilling to feel them in my heart and release them with my breath while tending to everyone before myself. Now was my time to connect with my heart free of any distraction.

My cup was finally empty. I filled it with the love of the Divine Mother in each meditation practice and discussion we had. I was aware of this blissful joy that's the nature of what we are and that always resides within us but was unable to locate from a mental space in the vibration of overwhelm and feeling of not good enough. This space within my vessel gave me the opportunity to see and feel the blessing that I am. I saw just how long I was running this automatic program of being not good enough. I was no longer looking or judging me from the pain of the ego mind. Waves of sadness came over me to be released. Tears flowed through me as I wept and released this default program. Divine Mother held me. I honored myself and saw myself in my heart.

Now that I had this space, I recalled an experience I had several years back. I attended a consciousness class with a friend. We all sat in a circle and were given an exercise to sing from our hearts. How we sounded did not matter, but the resonance from our being did. I couldn't get it no matter how hard I tried. My heart was so boarded up beneath locks and chains of self-judgment all my mind would do was force the words out louder. That was not the way in, and the facilitator knew it.

My cover was blown. I was asked to repeat, "I am a gift and a contribution to anyone lucky enough to be in my presence." Words I could not choke out without pain and tears. My heart ached for my own love and acknowledgment, but at that time, I was unwilling to release my suffering and receive my love and the infinite love of Source that has always been available whenever I chose.

For years, I'd utter those words, always with tears. But now from this space of open, clean, and clear, I selected wisely what I would refill my cup—my vessel, my self—with. I chose to declare my presence as a gift and a contribution not only to anyone lucky enough to be in my presence but first and foremost to ME! My love for me would fill my heart, so it was now my heart that was overflowing with LOVE instead of the ego overwhelmed, forever busy, and burdened with self-judgment and riddling my days with fear.

With the practice and presence of self-love, I became aware of my resilience and the power of choice I had to persevere through whatever challenge or obstacle was before me despite the judgments I was projecting on myself. As I looked back, I saw I had used these powers so many times before, and it provided me with so many blessings, but what I observed was it was with conscious choice that these blessings appeared abundantly. When things were difficult, I noticed I was controlling outcomes or resisting love—i.e., having self-judgments and limitations.

Back at work, I needed to course correct to function differently. I knew I needed to have space to connect within regularly to maintain my inner harmony, my connection to my heart, and my connection to Divine Mother. I began to set boundaries—not for myself, but from others and how I let them affect me. It wasn't personal. It was self-love. It was a conscious choice.

My schedule was mine to recreate. I'd stay on it honoring myself with time in nature, space between clients and appointments, not taking work home with me, daily personal time, and regular self-care. Then from time to time, I'd unconsciously let boundaries dissolve, and the old overdoing habits would creep in. Along with it came signs of becoming overwhelmed, but not as much self-judgment. I had given myself permission to have infinite do-overs. I would actually shake my hands as if I were holding an Etch-A-Sketch toy and allow myself to begin anew with a fresh breath in and with laughter. It was okay to make mistakes now, but it was not okay to remain in the suffering of the mistakes.

Choosing to walk a path of love and releasing limitation and fear had allowed me to plant seeds of infinite possibilities and give space to patience to allow the fruit to ripen. Since choosing to create boundaries, I now live by a no-plan Sunday rule.

However, one Sunday last spring, despite my resistance, I was guided by my heart to take a drive and follow a sign I recalled seeing. This wandering soon revealed a highly visible professional office space grounded with a giant, old oak tree out front and surrounded by nature. This space that I had passed hundreds of times, if not thousands, had been on the market for almost two years and was now available for half the asking price. Despite my rising fears, I kept following the yes' dispelling my limitations. In just over three months, I held the keys to my own space to recreate Garden of Life Massage and my dream life. The Garden rang in the new decade with ease, and I surrendered what no longer served me, overwhelm, and any belief that I was not enough.

The Source shows me that I am fully loved and supported when I choose my heart as my copilot. Choices are easy. I have time and space for all the things I love in my life. My work is abundant, successful, and it fuels me just as much as my playtime. My days are now mine. They begin with me connecting to my heart wandering in wonder with time in nature or on my yoga mat, or even better, doing yoga in nature.

Now I am able to serve my clients as an instrument with the love of Source flowing through me and have the time and space to be creative to invite in possibilities for growth and expansions that serve me and my community joyfully. I felt my True Power when I began to let go of control and fear and just listen to what my heart tells me and trusting it.

LIVING IN YOUR TRUE POWER

I Am the Answer

Heather Ann Fink

How did I get here? And how do I get out?

After an entire day in the emergency room, waiting to be seen by the doctor, I still wonder if this is the right place for me to be. I've been stripped of all my personal belongings and dressed in a hospital gown, and now I sit here feeling so embarrassed to be at such an extreme low and nervous for the next step. After trying an endless number of things on my own, with no success, I've agreed to give this a try, desperate to figure out how to change my life. With my mom by my side, we cry together through my fears and apprehension at the edge of what's next.

Finally, the emergency room physician is ready to meet me, and he talks me through the steps of admitting myself into the psychiatric unit. He lays out a very dull, bleak picture of how long I might be there, what the days would look like, and what the medication options are. Nothing about it actually gives me hope besides the fact that it's a plan.

My mom and I sit listening to this bleak description, staring at each other with a sense of uncertainty, when we are startled by the sound of a woman screaming just outside the door. She screams uncomprehendingly, as if from the bottom of a pit that has no escape. We hear her struggling and screaming as the hospital staff pulls her away. The levels of panic and anxiety in my body already present spike even higher and stay elevated while the physician informs us nonchalantly that, yes, I would indeed be in the psychiatric ward with this woman and other people in a similar state.

At this moment, it's crystal clear that admitting myself to the psychiatric unit is definitely *not* the help I'm seeking. The doctor delivers additional information: this *is* the only option he knows for me and for others needing similar support and guidance. *What?* I feel as if I've been punched simultaneously in my gut *and* in my heart—dumbfounded, disappointed, and ultimately left without a next step to get the help I came here for. I turn toward my mom, and my stomach and heart sink even deeper feeling her despair and grief at the end of this long haul with me. It's unreal these are the options for mental health in America.

*

When I was twenty years old, I met the man I would partner with until I was forty. The first five years of this twenty-year relationship exceeded all my expectations. I felt so lucky to meet a man like Zach—smart, charismatic, a natural leader, and very handsome. His confidence was such a comfort to me, and he seemed to know how to handle life in a way I had never experienced. I loved his family, they loved me in return, and I felt safe and cared for. We bought a house and adopted two dogs. Throughout our life together, we held a commitment to each other that we would be friends and family no matter what happened, and I believed it. I banked on it. I was all in.

But after about eight years into our partnership, I began to recognize I wasn't quite happy, certainly not as happy as he was. I identified I had some personal healing to do and began a path that led to a lifelong spiritual journey. My life and our relationship began to change.

I began to see our relationship from a larger perspective and noticed we had quite painful communication and power dynamics, and that Zach's behavior was very intimidating. The same pattern would happen repeatedly, like the time we were driving in the car and catching up on our design for the new fence we were building in the front yard.

The conversational flow comes to an abrupt halt when, once again, his feelings are hurt, and I feel my stomach sink and my breathing constrict in anticipation of where the conversation will go next. With each word I utter, he becomes more aggravated, and I find myself in the position of defending myself. Even though this pattern is not new, the intensity of emotion and a sense of urgency from Zach absorb my attention.

He delivers the familiar phrase: "I'm so offended you would say that."

Then I'm trying to figure out the magic words to say that will shift the uptick of tension. But I'm not able to make him feel any better. As usual, my explanation is making him more aggravated by the moment, and no matter what I say, it's never the right thing.

His temperature rises higher and higher until he yells, "Goddammit!" and punches the dashboard in an explosion of frustration.

In my head, I think, *Oh my god, seriously?* Now there's not only a permanent dent in the dashboard of our car but also nowhere to go with our conversation. So, like always, I cry. I'm not scared of him hurting me, but I'm intimidated I may lose our relationship.

In the aftermath of his blown temper, I sit sunken with heavy sadness, trying to figure out what I've said that made him so mad and how to avoid it next time. I search my memory of the event for my misstep, and I think maybe he's right to be offended, maybe I'm just making things harder than they need to be with all my explaining. My brain hurts, and I don't understand, but I'm determined to make our relationship work.

I didn't recognize how perfectly I played into his manipulation, and I wouldn't know the term for his behavior until several years later: *gaslighting*. I was a perfect match for the manipulative tactic of gaslighting because I was taught from childhood to question my ability to make good choices and seek answers outside of myself. Such a painful recipe.

I was motivated to adapt to his paradigm because I believed he knew better than me. I aimed to heal the "deficient" parts of me so that I could stand along with him on the pedestal I put him on. I banked on our relationship bringing me the love, joy, and happiness I wanted, and I became so dependent on Zach and our relationship for *my* success and well-being that I was at his mercy.

In hopes of change, I dove into therapy, support groups, and spiritual training. While I developed a deeper connection with myself than I had ever known, the divide between Zach and I grew deeper and wider. I was inspired to incorporate the depth of connection and ecstatic experiences I was discovering through my healing into our relationship, but Zach acted burdened by my deepening self-awareness, and it became clear we were not moving in the same direction together.

Twenty years later, I found myself repeatedly crying to him about the lack of connection, care, and quality time that we experienced together. It was clearer than ever that I was not experiencing the depth of intimacy I desired. Despite my requests and attempts, nothing changed, and I was met with the same intimidation tactic, like the moment in the car when he punched the dashboard: "Why can't you be grateful for what we have!" I could no longer continue with the dynamics at play between us and told Zach that I decided to back up and allow space and time for our relationship—and for me.

Despite our commitment to each other to remain friends and family, Zach told me I would have to move out. I felt such hurt and abandonment deeper than ever before. I was heartbroken at the loss of the loving connection we once had and my vision of being stronger together into the future after all this time. The act of moving out began a personal journey beyond anything familiar to me, and I descended into an experience that would be termed "a dark night of the soul." As our commitment dissolved, I felt the pain of losing everything, and the ground I stood on was liquefied.

Over the next several months, I became increasingly agitated and fearful and experienced a steady decline in my capacity to function normally. I spiraled deeper into disorientation and could not relate to the high-functioning self I had known. I did not feel safe, and a rigid fear took charge of my entire being. All the healing work and tools I had learned were inaccessible, and the intensity reached such a peak that I was unable to work, and I took several months away. Because my body was in an extreme state of panic and fear, I lost a shocking amount of weight and began experiencing panic attacks for the first time in my life.

I felt so agitated in my own skin that it distracted me from even making the next choice, finding myself pacing back and forth when I was alone. I was experiencing intense panic every moment of my day.

I tried what felt like every natural remedy and modality available in the oasis of my healing community and still found myself completely spun out and defeated. When the intensity peaked and prevented me from being able to relax and let go in my own body, I only slept three hours per night for over a month.

It was at this point of despair and defeat that I reluctantly agreed to follow the concerned requests of the women who loved me, and so I looked for help at the emergency room psychiatric unit.

Having searched for help but finding nothing that worked, I yearned to feel the old version of me that was so capable and high-functioning. I was desperate to feel myself again and get a foothold, at least for a minute to re-inhabit this capable version of me I knew before. I decided living with Zach again was a place to begin because when I was with him, I could recognize myself. I pitched the idea, and he reluctantly agreed.

After moving in with Zach, I experienced a shocking tragedy with Alejandro, one of my dearest friends. When he did not arrive to work for our regular Sunday shift together, I reached out and texted our mutual friends to check on him. I was sent into a haze of shock when I learned he had suffered a heart attack that morning while driving his car and collided head-on into a cement median. He was unconscious at the scene of the accident and was being held in a medically induced coma in the hospital. This beautiful man who was a treasured source of support and love of mine now lay in a hospital bed with an uncertain prognosis that he would live, be able to speak, sing opera, and dance again with his innate flair and passion. I went to the hospital, held his hand, cried, and spoke to him of the inspiration and love and miracle that he is—reminding him of his power and offering my pure care and love.

As days went by, the hospital limited visitors to one primary caretaker, and so one dear friend took the responsibility to stay by his side and update us daily on his developments.

A few days later, I was standing in Zach's kitchen, reading the latest update about Alejandro's status on my phone. Feeling vulnerable and tender, I stood in deep grief, connecting energetically with him in a state of medically induced coma in the hospital. I was able to feel and receive the overflowing love and warmth that he generated continually, and I felt *my* heart warm and full of love and care for my beautiful dear friend, and I felt our love for each other. Amazing.

In the loveliness of this sacred moment, Zach walked over to stand beside me, and I experienced an extreme contrast.

As I showed him the update, his response to me was of ice. Cold. Flippant. Callous. Careless.

He uttered the words, "Who knows what will happen?" in a tone that means he doesn't really care what happens. I was repulsed.

And ultimately, this clarity was exactly what I needed.

As I looked at him standing there, I was finally able to see who he really was, beyond the fog, behind the curtain, and in sharp focus—and inside, I think, "Wow, THERE you ARE! You're a cold hollow shell! Got it!" I'd been trying to mimic *this callous behavior* and idolizing his capacity to handle life "so well," but I finally understood that I'd *actually* been learning from Zach over all these years to have a cold, callous approach to life!

In this magical moment, I understood his way of living was never meant for me. I was not cold, flippant, callous, or careless, and I cannot live with my heart shut down. I cannot suppress the love that fills and bursts beyond my heart, and I don't want to.

That potent moment of being saturated in the flow of love between Alejandro's heart and mine brought me home to the warmth and freedom my heart was made for, and I felt the room I needed to breathe. This moment made clear all my confusion. This feeling was so powerful that it outshone any other choice or internal struggle that had stood in my way up until now.

Shortly after that day, I moved out for good, without a doubt that I would never live with him, sleep in the same bed, or have sex with him *ever* again.

It was done.

And I was clear.

Twenty years of gaslighting and crazy-making compromised my sanity. I recognized it was thinking "I'm crazy" that was the problem. I had believed "I would be crazy to listen to my own heart," but at this point in my journey, I knew it was the most important wisdom to listen to one's heart. I committed to choose what felt right for *me* and get hands-on experience responding to *my heart's wisdom.*

In the days that followed, I began embracing the love in my heart and moving toward what aligned with this warmth in my life. I began a moment-to-moment experience of choosing to love again and again and again. This became the first step of several on my path of liberation. Every layer of growth and healing after this point allowed more courage to make bigger choices, and my life unfolded into more potency and vibrancy, setting me free onto *my* path.

*

It's four years after the breakup. I'm now in a romantic relationship with Jimmy, and we've been together for two years.

Because he loves to serve me, I ask for his help with a tech issue I cannot figure out. As we're on my computer, I recognize our interaction has shifted out of being enjoyable, and I wonder why our exchange feels stressful and annoying for me; I feel him speaking to me like I'm a burden.

In the moment of disagreement, I'm no longer afraid to speak my heart and mind—to fully express myself without hesitation and stand in my love for myself! I'm clear that if it doesn't work for me, then it doesn't work for me, and I'm completely uninterested in manipulating myself to fit into any relationship!

I share with him how I'm feeling, "Why did you say that? What are you trying to do? Whatever you're trying to do right now is not helpful."

He gets calm and listens to me more; he pauses to assess his words and actions. He acknowledges, "Yeah, I can see how that would be annoying. I'm sorry. I didn't mean that. I won't say that anymore." He allows space for the energy of our interaction to shift and asks, "What would be better for you? Show me how you'd like it." He doesn't try to tell me that I'm wrong; he doesn't want to argue. He *wants* to know when his behavior upsets me because he wants to be with me, and he wants *me* to be happy with *him*. And my desire to be with him *is* reaffirmed because I feel heard, and I'm being loved, cared for, and supported.

The biggest reason this is so different is because *I've* changed. I get to have relationships like this now because I have this amazing relationship with myself! I do what I want, and I choose what's joyful for me. I feel happier, freer, and more liberated than ever in my entire life. I'm actually living in alignment with the wisdom of my soul, which is a freedom deeper than

I've ever known possible, and my heart's expression feels totally unobstructed and free to love all the way. Whew! I'm not trying to be anybody but myself, which makes my life and my relationships a lot easier.

Whereas I used to look to others for safety, success, and wholeness, now relationships are about being resourced in our own wisdom and exploring this with each other. I regularly step back and assess if the relationships in my life are serving me and my heart. I'm choosing partnerships that are empowering for everyone and choosing people who are already enjoying their own life.

True power for me is knowing the deep desires I feel in my heart are actually my guidance, in service to me, showing me the life I'm meant to have. My deeper heart's desires are *real* and lead me to the life I get to live and enjoy!

I am my own answer, just as every one of us is our own answer! I celebrate this truth that we are all equipped with innate guidance and true power from the very beginning, and all we ever need is right here within us! How exciting to have our own unique divine adventure waiting right here within our hearts!

Emptiness Filled

Gale Ziccarelli

Dear God,

Thank you for my innocent childhood. Thank you that I grew up in a white, middle-class family in the suburb of a Midwestern town. For giving me loving, caring parents and family. Thank you for making me feel safe and protected as a child. But, God, something went wrong! Was part of it the fact that women were powerless in the '50s and '60s when I grew up? Or that society at that time said men had all the power and women needed to please their man, and I bought into those beliefs? Or was it me and my choices, or am I just defective?

It's a Saturday morning in the '90s much like any other Saturday morning. I'm living in a four-thousand-square-foot house with a pool in suburbia in a medium-sized Midwestern town. I'm married to a psychiatrist and have two teenage boys. My husband is at work, which is his life, and the boys are in their rooms down the hall playing video games. I'm the office manager at an outpatient psychiatric clinic that my husband

and I own. I know nothing about running a business and have no desire to do so—this was my husband's dream, not mine. I have my bachelor's degree in social work. But somehow, I find myself in an emotionally abusive marriage with two children to take care of and a business to run.

Sitting in the upstairs bathroom, I'm crying my eyes out, but also trying not to make too much noise as to not alarm my boys. I pretend to be taking a bath and put on some loud music. I notice the rust-flowered wallpapers are stiff from hair spray. This formal, old-fashioned bathroom was decorated by the previous owner, and even it does not reflect me or my taste at all. Just as looking in the mirror right now I see a reflection of someone I no longer recognize. The loud music is drowning out my emotions. The emptiness inside of me is so real I imagine that I can almost touch it. I feel the cold, sterile feeling of the bathroom much like my cold, lifeless life. The walls seemed to be closing in on me as I sob and feel myself going numb. I have felt lonely and empty most of my marriage, but today is different. I find it ironic that I have the house, the husband, the children, the money, and the vacations, but none of it matters because I feel no love from my husband or for myself. Part of me feels guilty for wanting an escape from my life. Today, I feel so trapped that for a brief moment, I wonder if my life is worth living. But I think who would take care of my boys? The mere thought of what I'm thinking in this moment sends a wave of shock throughout my body. The shock scares me enough to bring me back to reality, and I know I need to get out of my marriage now!

Dear God,

How did I get here to this cold, sterile bathroom? What happened to that independent woman that I was in college before I met my husband? What happened to the young woman who dreamed of going to the Peace Corps before she met her husband? I fear I have lost her completely, and I'm afraid I can never get her back. Why did I give away a precious part of me for the sake of being loved? Why did I waste all those years trying to please my husband, my kids, and everyone else? Why am I even here?

I know I have a purpose, but I'm not seeing it in this moment, in this bathroom, when I'm crying and feeling so empty inside. So shattered, so hollow from giving away all the best parts of me. Do I matter? Does my life matter? Will my life ever get better?

I feel I have nothing left to give to anyone and certainly nothing to give to myself. The years of emotional abuse from my husband, the years of people-pleasing and trying to be the perfect doctor's wife and mother have taken a toll on me and my body. What am I to do, God/Source/Creator of all that is? I'm afraid to leave my husband, afraid he will find a way to take the kids from me. I'm afraid I won't be able to provide for my kids, and they will resent me. I'm afraid, I'm afraid, I'm afraid. And there is no one here to help me but you!

Suddenly, I'm jolted back to reality when one of my sons calls my name. "Mom, I need you!" So I wipe my eyes and act like nothing has happened, like I always do. I put a smile on my face and try to pretend that I'm whole, but I know inside I'm not. The desperation I feel today in this bathroom and the thoughts of wondering why I'm here and what is the purpose of even being here have scared me enough. I know I have to make some major life changes. But what? I feel like there is no reply from God.

At first, I just went back to my life. Then one day, my husband and I are at a cocktail party in Chicago at one of the doctor's homes. I'm trying to fit into the mold of the upper-class doctor's wife that I had been thrown into several years before. My husband and I socialize, but then later in the evening, I find myself alone with one of the wives. This woman asks me a simple question about my opinion on a certain matter. My mind just goes blank, searching for an answer, but no words come out of my mouth. Now I no longer remember what the topic of conversation was with this woman, but it does not matter.

However, her question starts a flood of awareness within me. I discover I have formed very few opinions of my own up to this point in my life even though I'm in my forties. I eventually come to the full realization that I have learned to filter everything I think through the lens of what my husband would want rather than forming my own opinions. I also have the awareness that I have been filtering my thoughts through those of my parents too. This is a shocking knowledge, and in this moment, I'm even made more aware of what an empty shell I have become—a fragile, empty shell where very little of my former self still exists (or no self at all). I do not know how at this time, but I know I have to save myself and find that old self who once existed.

It takes me another year, but with the help and guidance from another psychotherapist who is my mentor, I've become strong enough to ask my husband for a divorce. My mentor builds up my self-esteem and helps me see other areas in my life where I'm already powerful, which gives me hope. I have always wanted to go back to school to get my master's degree in social work, so after the divorce, I return to school and eventually become a psychotherapist. I find that all my years of life experience make me an even better therapist. I'm a little late returning to college since, by now, my oldest is just starting college himself, but I'm finally putting my needs first for once! These first few years after the divorce and graduate school are not easy, but I'm finally finding my power again, and that feels wonderful.

I continue on my journey, and I come to the knowing that we all have a beautiful eternal flame inside of us that lives and grows in us. We need to tend to that flame because that flame is precious, and it is our life force, our soul, our essence. If we ignore it, it does not burn as brightly, and if we give it too much fuel, we combust. Our task is to neither let negative nor positive words, people, things, or actions outside us influence (affect) our flame. It is our flame, only our flame.

I'm learning to tend that flame inside of me with meditation, patience, and love for myself. As I do, my flame grows stronger, and it becomes a steady source of support. That source of support is what I have needed all along. It is not the love and acceptance of others—it is my love I need, my own guidance and support, and nothing outside of me can give that to me. I have found my true power, it is me and my connection to Source.

I get myself out of a marriage where I never felt valued, and now I find myself in a job where I do not feel valued either. Again, I feel powerless. I'm starting to set better boundaries with others, but evidentially, I still have more lessons to learn. I realize my flame is starting to grow dim again. I'm giving too much of myself—emptying myself out—to my job and my clients. So I decide to quit my job, and I go on a yoga retreat and find myself again in a bathroom pleading with God. I know something has to change, and again the answer I get is *me*.

I decide to take a year off and work on my physical health and reconnect with myself again. But this time, I'm also starting to connect with Spirit. I'm using the word *Spirit* now because I know a lot of people are turned off by the word *God*. I too have trouble relating to formal religion myself. But I now realize I can connect to Spirit anywhere. It does not have to be in a stuffy church on a particular day at a particular time. Spirit now becomes a source of support that is with me at all times in all places. So I went on a quest to rediscover myself after my divorce.

Looking back, I see that I've spent twenty-three years in an emotionally abusive marriage where I kept trying to twist myself into something else hoping it would please my husband and children. But it never worked, and in the process, I lost myself, my identity, my soul. I now feel powerless—truly powerless. Real love, I did not realize at that time, does not require me losing myself. I blame others in my life for not giving me the love I need, but eventually, I come to the awareness that it is me who is not loving me. I have not been open to receiving their love. It is like I have posted a big yellow CLOSED sign on my heart, so of course, no love is allowed in. But I'm hopeful I will eventually learn to open my heart and take down that CLOSED sign.

During my marriage and for a few years after my marriage, I'm caught in the cycle of seeing myself as a victim. Even though I'm a therapist, I still have a blind side to my own problems. It is easy now to blame everybody outside of me rather than look at my own issues. That is what keeps me in the cycle of blame, repeat, blame! But luckily, I love reading self-help books and taking courses to improve myself so I explore different ideas and find what works for me. Now I'm able to give up seeing myself as a victim, and I'm slowly starting to see myself as a victor instead.

I discovered one of the things I lost along the way was my connection to my inner child. That inner part of me was feeling sad, lonely, empty, and afraid. She needed my attention and love. She needed to know I was there for her no matter what. She was like a lost part of me with which I had to reconnect. So I loved and nurtured my little one, and eventually, she started to feel whole again.

I start learning more about my own energy in the classes I'm taking. I now know that my energy is *my* energy, and I don't have to give it away to others. By learning to control my energy, I can shift my reality from the inside out. After one of the classes I attended, I have this clear knowing that I'm supposed to stop doing psychotherapy and do something else. So I follow my knowing and take a leap of faith—not knowing where I'm heading. I had been practicing as a psychotherapist for years and loved mental health and helping people. But now I decide to leave the field of psychotherapy so that I can become a life coach and use the new skills I have learned.

About a year before I joined the life coaching program, I had known that I was supposed to be part of the next group, but I ignored the message. On the last day of the training I was attending, I was invited to lunch with a group of about ten people. When I got there, I realized everyone in the group was starting the coaching program the next year but me. Everyone was excited about the future, and I was a little jealous. But everyone was younger, and I was still working and had health issues, so I decided it was not a good time for me.

That following year, I had more health issues and struggles with my family. But then the next year, I did follow my intuition, and I joined the program. I felt very guided and supported and things just fell in place. When I stood up on the stage with all the new coaches and said yes to doing the program, it felt so empowering. I was finally standing up and saying yes to me for the first time in my life.

Part of me knew even in my lowest moments that I was destined for more—that I had a purpose, and now I get to live that purpose. I'm here to help others find their inner light and live their purpose.

Over the years, I spent so much time focusing on everything and everyone outside of me and ignoring my own self. If you peeked into my life at that time, you would have seen on the outside the perfect house and yard, nice clothes, cars, and great vacations.

Flash back. It's the '90s, and I'm waking up in my nicely decorated, spacious house and going for a swim in the pool. I plan our next vacation to the Bahamas. I take a drive in my sports car to do some casual shopping in Chicago. I'm a room mother at my kids' school, and I always say the right thing. But inside, I feel nothing.

Flash forward. It's 2020, and I'm standing on a mountaintop in Hawaii feeling the rain pour down on me, and I'm looking up at the beautiful rainbow stretching all the way across the sky. The rainbow is so close it feels like I can almost touch it. I think I must be in heaven, but then I realize this is just my life now.

I notice the stillness in the air, and it feels like life as I know it has stopped for just a moment. My past no longer exists, and my future has not yet begun. So all I have is this Now. I notice my breath—slow, calm, and steady—and feel my center. I'm truly present in this moment, in my body, taking in all the sounds, scents, and tastes around me.

I feel the presence of Source all around me—in the taste of the water on my lips and the beautiful scent of the flowers and the lush vegetation all around me. I'm dressed casually for comfort, and I don't care that my hair is wet and my makeup is running, I feel alive now—truly alive.

I'm with a group of fellow life coaches, and I can just simply be myself. We have been on lots of magical adventures together traveling to Sedona, Mt. Shasta, and other places together. I feel a strength from within that guides my words and actions now. I'm stable, grounded, and I'm in bliss. I look forward to the future with excitement and anticipation of what is to come and what I am to become. My inner guidance is propelling me forward now in ways I could have never imagined. I don't always know where I'm going, but I know the path is divine. Life is no longer a struggle but a wild adventure to be experienced.

Dear Spirit,

It's me again. Thank you that I now feel whole, complete, and happier and more fulfilled than I ever have in my life. Thank you that I now have friends and family who I love and who love me back. Thank you that I'm able to wake up each day and be grateful for what I already have, and I can look forward to a future with so much hope and excitement. Thank you that my body is now healthy, and I feel alive. Thank you that I have gotten to travel to faraway places and I now can connect with people on such a deep level. Thank you that I now truly love and value myself and my life and now I can teach this to others as a life coach.

The Best Is Yet to Come

Aurora Hood Hammond

It's a very hot, humid morning, the middle of summer in Sydney, Australia. I'm already out of breath, running late for work. As I grab my things to leave the house, my phone rings. I hear the voice of my son, Daniel, as I get in the car.

He's in tears, speaking fast and uncontrollably, with lots of swearing. It's terrible to listen to. My heart is breaking as I hear the panic in his voice and think of the year we've spent trying to get his life on track and how exhausted by it all we feel. The tirade of negativity and despair continues blasting in my ears.

I come to a stop at the top of the drive. My neighbor is waiting to turn in. There's another car coming down the narrow street. The other drivers are looking at me, and I can't figure out what to do. I know I'm the one blocking traffic, but I'm frozen. I can't think or process what needs to happen. I'm not aware of how long I've been sitting there. Eventually, someone blasts their horn. In confusion, I just start driving up the hill; someone else must have moved.

For the first time in his thirty-two years of life, I tell Daniel on the phone, "I just can't help you right now," and hang up. I pull over and burst into dark, heavy sobbing. I have a client waiting for me at the office, and I'm late.

I'm a mental health professional, and this is the state I'm in! A wave of fear engulfs me. I feel shock with the thought, *Oh, no, I can't be here again!*

It's been ten years since the Great Breakdown of 2008—the depression, financial collapse, loss of a business, loss of a relationship, the list goes on. For the first time in young Daniel's life, there's no more school, and life as an adult on the autism spectrum has truly begun. And guess what? It's worse than the life as a child with a place to go every day and somewhere to be given direction. In adult life, there are no more teachers, no more safe environment, no more structure, and no more uniform to wear.

For the first time since then, I can't pick up the slack and figure out the next move. I'm exhausted and out of ideas—again.

That last episode of burnout and depression took us a good two years to work our way through, during which time I couldn't work or pay bills. I don't know what to do; I can't think. My brain is not functioning, my heart palpitating. My crying is out of control.

I remember my surprise the week before when a friend pointed out to me that I didn't seem okay. I felt my fragility as soon as she pointed it out! She had said, "Call me anytime."

The vulnerability of a lifelong care-giver tends to go unnoticed by most, including the care-giver themselves. It's hard to know if you are burning people out when they ask how you are, and the story just falls out of you.

You lose all perspective of a normal conversation. Then you start staying quiet, just to be sure.

Feeling desperate, I remember my friend's recent invitation. I have never called her before (as to not burn her out). I pick up the phone.

Thank God she picks up! I can feel her caring for me. She reminds me I'm not alone—that help and support are possible. She also reminds me I'm loved by a higher source of power. That it's possible to find my way through this with Love rather than struggle to do it all myself as I've done all my life.

I start to feel the energy as she's speaking to me, and I know that something else is possible; I don't have to go back to my old patterns or be a victim of my situation anymore.

I have understood this in theory for a while, and now I really need to put it into practice.

The lead up to this moment was that Daniel had moved out of our home three months before. He wanted to move in with his fiancé to try living independently. To get this far, it had taken government-funding interviews, a year of meetings, talking with support workers, plus being woken up at 1:00 a.m. on most nights due to his anxiety or mine. *Now it's all falling apart!*

His support worker had found an apartment for him to live in near his fiancé's home, across the road from a golf course (one of his obsessions). I stayed over the first night in his new place to help him settle in. His fiancé came to stay the second night. They were both in tears, very anxious. I cooked them dinner, tucked them into bed, and watched TV until they fell asleep. I cried all the way on the one-hour drive home.

For three very up-and-down months, Daniel cooked and cleaned, worked, went to yoga, walked by the river each day, and tried to encourage his fiancé to join him in their nest. She chose the placemats and bed linen, bedside tables, and vases and seemed to be having fun and take pride in their achievements. But every few days, she said goodbye to him and went home to Mum and Dad! Because of that, Daniel became more and more frustrated—then angry. He pursued her home, nagged and cajoled, which did not help her anxiety. He was obsessed. Eventually, he lost it, her dad lost it back, and the rest, as they say, was history. Breaking their engagement, she called off the seven-year relationship they had both depended on. He was devastated. We walked and talked. I was so sad it had ended like this. What was going to happen now?

I am standing in my kitchen when my friend and neighbor Ellen asks me, "What are you going to do if Daniel wants to move home?"

I'm amazed to hear the absolute certainty and confidence in my answer: "We are moving to the Sunshine Coast!" She looks at me in shock. I have been feeling the call to this part of the world for nearly three years, ever since a wise friend who lives there said, "You should come and live up here." In that moment, much to my surprise, I had felt a huge YES in my system, but could not imagine how that could come to pass.

Wow! I'm stunned. That's a huge interstate move that requires buying and selling houses and packing up my already overwhelming house and life. That feels like a really big mountain to climb, and I'm already stressed and exhausted.

Yet the energy coming through with that statement shakes me to the core, with excitement! Excitement—that's something I haven't felt in a very long time!

It feels like doors are flying open in the Universe, and a great wind is blowing through. How can I already know that it feels so good? Yet I do.

My spiritual path has meant that for decades; I have practiced meditation and sought out teachers and communities to support me with understanding the challenges in my life. I have also learned to fine-tune and develop my capacity for intuition and access the higher mental faculties for guidance. Having had posttraumatic stress disorder since the age of twelve when my older brother died, and I nearly died six weeks later, my brain has been anxious and unregulated through no fault of my own. I have been labeled and thought of myself as neurotic, a drama queen, too sensitive—the list goes on. My anxiety has led to postpartum depression and had a big impact on Daniel as well. I was a single mother for the first four years of his life, and it was not an easy time.

Finally, as part of my practice as a clinician, I realized the depth of the PTSD I've endured. It has inevitably added extra challenges to being the parent of a child on the autism spectrum before that was understood in the 1990s. (In the 1980s, it was all my fault because I was a single mother!)

I have a trick or two up my sleeve for taking on life-changing moments like this. I know that the first step is to buy myself time in which to regroup and gather some life force for this momentous move to go into action.

Therefore, I ask my son if he can keep it together for two weeks while I go to Hawaii to be with Rikka Zimmerman and the Life Transformed Coaching community. (Bless him, he knows it is the best hope for us both!) "Yes, mum," he says.

I arrive in Hawaii barely able to speak or look anyone in the eye. The magical beauty of the island of Maui, the daily immersion in the teachings, the inspirational company, and breathing in the love for six days do the trick. Sitting on the deck of the whale-watching boat in the setting sun, with the vivid beauty of the Hawaiian mountains at my back, life feels full of deep joy and promise.

I've always known that accessing our true power is a matter of alignment with the Source/Soul presence within us. I've practiced developing that alignment in many ways, mainly meditation, and have had some amazing experiences. This situation feels like I'm going to need every skill of alignment I've ever known.

So I come home to stare at the impossible-looking mountain in the face.

I know the move needs to happen fast. Asking a person on the autism spectrum who is already distressed to adapt to this much change is huge. We need to get the ball rolling so he knows what's to come. Interesting! Because I have no idea!

Like many on the spectrum, Daniel has a very clear knowing of what is a YES in his life, as well as what is a NO. I trust his internal sense of knowing.

When he looks up at me tearfully one day and says, "Oh, mum, what are we going to do?" I reply without hesitation, "We are moving to the Sunshine Coast." He simply nods—I can feel his YES.

We all love reading accounts of the miracles of synchronicity, confirmation, and magic that are possible from being truly in the flow. I wish I had time to tell you about all of them; there are just so many amazing things that happened. It's not about making the right decision or even being clear.

It is about being in the highest energy we can access at the time and being open to the guidance.

How do you do that when you are already running on empty? I didn't know the answer to that question. I wasn't clear how to get all this to happen—I did know I wasn't on my own. My divine Source is always with me.

I literally had to surrender and let go and allow the mountain to move itself. I simply couldn't control or orchestrate all the things that needed to come together in a very short time. And so the sit-down, lie-down method of getting things done is born!

The first step is to fly to the Sunshine Coast; it's an hour-and-a-half flight north of Sydney to tropical Queensland. The second step is to buy a house—we need to know exactly where we are going! Somewhere in my meditation, the question arises: what am I looking for?

I receive the inspiration that it's possible to find an acre of land with a cottage and a shed and have two living spaces separate and together. Perfect! Show me the way.

It's Easter, the time of magic and miracles. We fly north on Good Friday and have ten possible properties to view on Saturday. I ask the question: How will I know which one?

The answer: You will feel the Peace and the Love!

Okay! I'm good with that!

It literally is the first property, which I don't like particularly in the online pictures. It's a dimly lit, smelly house, with a lovely big shed, and as I step out into the overgrown yard and close my eyes, in comes a massive download of Peace and Love. I open my eyes in shock! It can't be this easy!

Then I see the circle of tall white gum trees, protected by a bamboo forest, and I start to tune into the magic that's here. Spring water coming up out of the ground fills the swimming pool, fairies laugh in the trees, and dragons are breathing nearby, I'm just sure. I feel my feet rooted to the ground, and I ask permission of the land to be on it.

"Yes!" is the resounding reply. "We are waiting for you." There is a sense of something ancient, the volcanoes that once filled this valley, an ancient knowing that includes me somehow. A living presence that recognizes and embraces me, a welcome in the sound of wind in the leaves of so many trees at once.

I have not had a true sense of place in any other home I have lived in. This is coming home to somewhere in my ancient past. I feel alive and uplifted. I know the support will be here.

So that is why, without finance, or having sold my Sydney house, or knowing much about how it's going to happen, I sign a contract. I return to Sydney the proud owner of a piece of tropical paradise.

Ellen, my neighbor, is shocked—again! The move is on, and the energy of the Universe is sweeping underneath my wings.

The sit-down, lie-down method for the exhausted looks like this: I have a to-do list, I plan for a day of packing. Then I discover I simply cannot function that day! I lie down, sometimes all day. Sit down, take a breath, don't make the phone call!

"How did it all get done?" I hear you asking.

Truthfully, I don't quite know. I would wake up in the middle of the night and get up and pack some boxes and make a phone call (the utility shops are open twenty-four hours and no waiting at 3:00 a.m.!). Then I would go back to sleep.

The other big learning was to allow myself to receive help. Like most people with childhood trauma, I've always been good at doing things on my own. People may offer, "Let me know if there's anything I can do," but it's hard to think of anything and then impossible to ask. So when my real estate agent just comes and clears out my garage, my neighbor cooks us food, and my friends come for the weekend and pack and label the boxes, I realize this is love in action. I have reached a place where I can allow this to happen for me.

The even bigger surprise! We had fun! There was laughter, coffee, sunshine, and support for me, my son, and Molly, our West Highland terrier. I just had to keep saying yes and allow it to flow.

As I lie on the couch and try not to panic about the packing that isn't being done, I can feel the magnitude of what's unraveling in my system. I'm preparing to leave the city of my birth, my family history, and my career, knowing I will never come back. All that I have will come with me, and that is the end. Bridges are burning.

I can truthfully say I never wavered in my decision for a moment. I could feel the Peace and the Love flowing into me whenever I thought of our new home. The land itself was calling me to a new way of being and a new life. *My true power is in me and all around me.*

Sometimes, as I am listening to the wild cacophony of native birds and opening the wide country gate on my gravel driveway, lined with palm trees, I think back to that moment in the driveway in Sydney. I take a huge breath and feel the smile on my face. Every time I drive out this gate, I feel excited and uplifted—truly! The beauty of the forest, the quiet of the road, the joy of driving anywhere up here—it's all so beautiful. I have been guided to people and places that welcome me and say, "We are so glad you are here!" I'm finding my tribe at last!

I feel so much gratitude for my ability to listen and to act. Listening to the miracles and guidance every step of the way got me here—even when it meant lying down and doing nothing! Developing my intuition through meditation and other practices has been the key to finding my True Power and stepping into my new life.

And the most unexpected miracle? Two weeks after arriving, we connect with amazing support. We meet the people from Sunshine Butterflies disability services, where Daniel finds a supportive community and a beautiful girlfriend who offer him a quality of life I never imagined possible. I had no idea this would be part of our new life! For the first time ever, I have real support with managing his needs and life with people who truly understand. No wonder the birds are singing!

The Sun Always Shines

Debbie Shuman Espinoza

Sitting here on the bunk in my prison cell, after another long, sleepless night, I feel the warmth of the sun rising through the bars of my window as the shadows dance across my legs. The silence of the prison is deafening; my thoughts are so loud in comparison. Utter despair takes over, and that familiar voice echoes in my head as it has every day since being here, *You always fuck up. Nothing you ever do is right.* These words constantly circle around in my head. My dad's face appears in my mind, and the words he speaks worsen my dreadful thoughts: *Debbie, you are so smart. What the hell are you doing with your life? You could have been an attorney. You could have had an amazing life. Look at you now.*

His words keep repeating in my head, they are so repetitive that I begin telling them to myself, with an emphasis that punches me in the gut. *What a complete waste of a life! You're a drug addict. Of all the places you could be, you're in a damn prison? What a complete fuck-up you are!*

All these words remind me of the disappointing daughter that I am. This sense of being unworthy has been long ingrained in me. Looking down at the shadows dancing on my legs, I mouth these hurtful phrases to myself yet again. The brick walls of my cell begin to close in on me, tighter and tighter, faster and faster. He is right, everyone is. All I ever do is hurt people. They're all better off without me.

The beautiful faces of my three children come into mind, and realization strikes me. Oh my God…what the fuck have I done? My kids are with some stranger. Are they scared? Is the stranger they are with hurting them? Do they cry for me at night wondering if I'll ever come home?

Maybe my kids are better off without me. My poor babies, I miss them so much. What an awful mom I am to put my kids through such trauma! I must fix this, for them, for me.

How do I fix this? I do not know what's happening. New voices swirl in my head, *Go to the church*. I don't understand. I don't believe in God, so why would I go to church?

My feet begin walking on their own. My steps lead me through the prison grounds. I see a multitude of suffering as I walk. These people before me are doing drugs, fighting, some just walking alone with their faces full of fear and despair. I see myself in all of them. I don't want to be them. I don't want this life anymore.

My feet keep walking. I'm flowing with them as they lead me down to this dilapidated building, which has become the prison church. I arrive as the service begins. Sitting in this pew, attempting to listen to the service, my mind remains blank. I still have no idea why I'm here, alone in this unfamiliar space. As I stare at the inmates around me, I notice they're different from the souls I just passed by. There's more in them; there's hope in their eyes. My body trembles, and I feel an unusual warmth inside me as this insurmountable presence of ease surrounds me. I've never felt such peace in my life. Is this what I've been missing?

Tears well up in my eyes and begin cascading down my face. There's a small flicker of hope in my heart, such a sharp contrast to the disparity that has become my world. I fall to my knees and pray. For the first time in my life, from the depths of my soul, I legitimately pray.

Oh, God, please save me…

Then the course of my life flashes before my eyes. It begins with my mother leaving me on a street corner when I am four. How scared I am on that huge corner with all the giant cars whizzing by me! As I watch her drive away, I cry to myself, "Mommy, please come back." But she never does. So how on earth can I love myself or have any sort of knowing of who I must be when my own mother doesn't want me? Who will ever want me if my own mother just throws me away?

Next comes my father's addiction, absence, and abandonment. Again, my well-being is disregarded. I'm just a shadow in the background of his drugs. I see my twelve-year-old self overdosing on his drugs. Even after this incident, he doesn't quit. What's the power these drugs have over him? Why does he love them more than his own daughter?

Now flash the good times with my father: my six-year-old self standing up in between the seats of our red VW van as I shift the gears for him. I feel the engine below me as it kicks into each gear, and away we go flying down the streets. Not a care in the world, my daddy and me! Oh, the love I feel for this man in this moment! But when I turned twelve, this closeness has dwindled; it has turned into endless attempts of me trying to earn back his love. I convince myself that by also taking drugs, I will make him love me as much as he loves them. How am I supposed to know my worth when neither of my parents knows theirs?

Still kneeling on the prison pew, I see that it was this same age when I had my first sexual encounter—in the arms of a thirteen-year-old boy. His clumsy touch and warm breath on my face try replacing the love I no longer receive. Gazing into his eyes, I see nothing. This is just an act for him. I am nobody. He rolls off me and gets up to play as I'm not even worthy of a kiss afterward. I think to myself, *Please, stay with me, love me. I just want to be seen, heard, loved.*

I now see myself at fourteen having my first abortion, and again at sixteen. These poor babies never had a chance. I'm so young and so scared, and this is not what I should be doing. I'm just a kid. How can I take care of a baby when I can't even take care of myself? I block this from my mind and continue life as if nothing's wrong, like nothing ever happened. As my life continues, the pain does too. I stuff the pain down with more boys, more drugs, and staying out all night looking for love—looking for myself. I cannot find either.

This is hard to relive. It all leads me down my own path of addiction. This addiction began to spiral after the death of my second husband, the love of my life, at the age of thirty-two. This is torture! I love him so much; he was supposed to be my answer.

The next recollection is of my third husband, who is physically and mentally abusive. I feel his hands around my neck as I am up in the air, my feet flailing. I cannot breathe. I look in his eyes and croak out the words, "My kids." Something snaps in him. I fall to the ground choking and sobbing. He spares my life for my kids, but maybe I deserve to be killed, especially by my husband.

My parents, my partners, no one wants me. My heart is beating a thousand times a minute as my entire life continues to flash before my eyes—the experiences, the smells, the memories...I never want to feel these emotions again. Why did all this happen? Why did everything I love leave me? What did I do wrong to deserve all this pain? It feels like everything I do in my life is wrong. I'm simply *wrong* in every way. How wrong am I as a child, to be unworthy of my parents' affection or anyone's affection?

As I stand up from the pew, wiping away my tears, I now understand there's not one specific turning point in my life that led to my wrongness or feeling unworthy— it has been all of it. All the pain and suffering, which originally led me down the path of addiction, also led me to find myself in this prison where I've reached my breaking point.

A few months later, I'm walking out of these prison gates. I hear the metal bars slam behind me; I know I'm never going back. Regardless of the obstacles lying ahead, nothing is going to stop me from living my destiny. No, I'm never going back. I take one last look at the sight of these formidable gates and barred windows, turn around, and take the first steps toward this choice of a new way of life.

Now out of prison, I'm back in this abusive relationship. I still believe I deserve this pain and abuse. I'm still living in a world consumed by my shame. Shame for everything "wrong" I've ever done in my life. I'm homeless (living in a tent in my sister's backyard). I thought things were going to change, but why am I still struggling so much?

That little prison church flashes in my mind, and for a moment, I can feel the peace and ease in every cell of my body. That flicker of light is still in me pulsating, calling for me, and I'm determined to help it burn brighter. I can no longer hide from my demons or push away my pain. I must face it all head-on. I'm scared to death to look so deep within myself—to feel all the guilt, shame, and pain I've caused myself and my family. It does not matter what people will say or think. I've changed inside, and now my outside must change as well. I want to live a life where I can feel that peace and ease—not only as a flicker, but as an eternal flame.

I cannot change this all on my own. I know I need some sort of help, but from whom? I'm still alone. I find myself at lunch with a dear friend I haven't seen in over fifteen years. She was the maid of honor at my first wedding, and we were once inseparable. I notice she has changed over the years; I see that spark in her eyes I want so desperately to have in my own. I break down in my desperation for change and confide in her, "I need help. I'm trying to do this alone, and I can't take another step forward. I'm stuck, and I need you, please help me."

She listens to me as I pour my heart out. She grabs my hand and says, "I'm willing to give you a part of my soul until you're strong enough to find yours again." After fifteen years, it's as if no time was ever lost between us. She's willing to give to me the love, reassurance, guidance, acceptance, compassion, and worth of which I'm incapable of giving to myself. I've asked for help, and here it is. This is the most profound beautiful gift anyone has ever given me.

Following that lunch, over the next few years, my light becomes radiant. I knocked down my walls and became vulnerable. I stopped playing the victim and started to take responsibility for my life. I begin to share my journey with others.

I'm ready to go on stage for the first time and share myself, to fully let the true light of me shine. Closing my eyes, I let the light of the Universe in through the crown of my head. The light radiates through me as I step on to the stage. Everything is still, and this voice from inside comes pouring through me. This voice is the voice of love, of compassion, the real *me*. It has never had the chance to be heard until this moment and tears fall from my eyes. This is who I'm meant to be, this is my purpose here in the world, and I am stronger than I ever dreamt possible.

As I built myself stronger, the relationships in my life started to improve. I now confront this man who has abused me for so long. I gather every ounce of strength and speak up for every part of me that has ever been scared, bullied, or put last, and say, "No more!" despite the possibility of him killing me. I shall at least go down fighting. I choose to leave the abuse; I choose to put all the wrong and unworthiness behind me. With all my heart, I choose to put myself first. I choose with every part of me that has ever put myself last or has been told I'm not good enough. I choose with my life. I choose me! I stand up to him and say, "I no longer deserve this abusive relationship. You have claimed so much of me for so long. I know I'm worthy of so much more than you." I see a flicker of realization in his eyes. This time he knows he cannot win—that I am done.

I now feel compassion for myself and what I have been through, which also allows me to feel compassion for my parents and this abusive man who has consumed my life for so long. I can see now that they did the best they could, and I will do the same. The cycle has been broken with me. I have claimed my worth.

Five years later

It's Saturday night, and I'm getting ready with my children. Tonight is very special. I've written a book titled *Wakening Your Worth*. This journey into unlocking the worthiness warrior within has become my calling. It's the celebration party in honor of this book hitting number 1 on the Amazon Best Seller list in three different categories. Looking down in the eyes of my three beautiful children, I'm overwhelmed with love. What amazing people they have become! I've put them through so much, yet here they are standing before me with such pride in their eyes. Wow, how did

I get to be so lucky? I've never felt more blessed than in this moment—that peace and ease have become my life.

"Congratulations, Mom! We are all so proud of how far you've come. You're the strongest woman we know. We love you."

I can't even hold back the tears. I—no, we did it together. We get in the car and go to my best friend's house. She has gone all out for this occasion, and I feel so special. This beautiful woman whom I once went to for help is now throwing me a celebration. Everything has come full circle. Walking into the room, I see it's filled with my friends and family. There's a special cake with the cover of my book on it, and the backyard is lit up like a fairy tale. As I step into the string lights, I realize all these people are here for me. I'm worthy of whatever the world has to offer *me*.

The day I gazed at the sun's dark shadows through my cell bars, I had not realized my life would soon be changed forever. My revelation came from sitting in a prison church pew. It was perfect for me to have that experience, so that now on the other side of all that unworthiness, I know I'm a divine gift, as this life is a divine gift. The day the sun shone on my face, through the bars of my cell window, my life changed forever.

I now *love* myself to the core. Have you ever had so much love for something in your life that there's this feeling that encompasses you and your heart feels so full it just might burst? That's how I now feel about myself and my life. I've turned my life from a tragic novel to a story of love, power, and worth. The girl in the beginning of this chapter, who once wanted to die because she felt so immensely unworthy, is now living a life of heaven on earth.

Oh my gosh, what a beautiful life this is! I write, I speak, I inspire. My days are now filled with so much love, acceptance, and purpose. I revel in the smallest things, the sun's warmth on my skin, the birds chirping in the sky; these have always been in the background of my life, but the sun has always been shining. I was just never able to see all the beauty life has to offer. I know in the deepest depths of my soul that I'm *worthy* of living life as the gift it's meant to be. There's no longer any of that old negative rumination. I've come to know that everything I went through was perfect. I'm a divine light here on earth to bring awareness to suffering and unworthiness. I rejoice in my journey and what it has been.

After going through all this and reaching my true power, I believe my true power is me and my worth, and I believe your true power is you and your worth as well. I hope my story showed you that you too have the power to change your life and become your own worthiness warrior—to live the life of your dreams.

I challenge you to step into those moments of pain and feel what has hurt you the most. Give voice to the shame you are feeling, which has controlled your life. Once we give a voice to our shame, it dies as worthiness rises. You are your own sun. You are as worthy in your darkness, as you are in your light. I challenge you above all else, to claim yourself because you are your own True Power!

Conclusion

Rise Higher in Your True Power

I f you have let yourself get soaked up in the immense life energies pulsating in these fourteen stories, then we hope you have also absorbed them into your own being. If we can do it, so can you! Starting now, infinite possibilities await you!

As depicted in fourteen different ways throughout this book, Your True Power is being your true self while in absolute alignment with Source. This source can be called Spirit, Energy, Universe, Being, Higher Self, God, Divine, Love, Light, Presence, Life Force, Creator, Consciousness, Christ Consciousness, Buddha Consciousness, the Quantum Field…

While everyone may interpret it or experience it differently, the main takeaway is that there is something infinite that encompasses all of life. I call it Source, the first mover, the origin of all that exists. But this Source has nothing to do with religious beliefs. It is beyond all the confines of religion. What you call it is personal to you, and it can even be deeply personal that you can make up your own name for it. Yet know that we are referring to the same Essence, the same Source.

In pure oneness in Source, you are all the love, all the possibilities, and all the power in existence. When you allow Source to flow through you and fill in the well of your being *as you* without separation, your struggle ceases to exist, and life is a layering of miracles in every moment.

Now that you've finished reading this book, you're now part of this ongoing story. Through these fourteen stories of transformation, you have walked through discovering, stepping into, and living in your true power. It is now time for YOU to go into happily ever after and rise higher in your true power!

Being in Your True Power is an ever-expanding journey. No matter how epic the previous moment has been, the next just gets better and better, going beyond what you can possibly imagine. Every problem turns into a joyful opportunity for growth, so you can experience more life, love, and abundance. Challenges are no longer something to be afraid of or avoid, but something to delight in, just like when you love the challenge of a marathon or getting to your thousandth yoga class. Nothing gets in your way or brings you down, for *anything that feels like any semblance of struggle isn't there to stop you, but rather it is coming up to leave so you can flow with greater ease.*

Everything is serving you for an ever-expanding realization of the infinite magical possibilities and bliss that are available to you. In Your True Power, you simply enjoy the constant awe of all the amazing things that unfold.

Bringing this book together at the onset of the global pandemic was not without obstacles. But we chose to unravel it all from the space of True Power. Old triggers around judgment, getting things done, writing our stories, visibility, marketing, and a magnitude of core issues arose. They came up because we were ready for more. When they appeared, we made them welcome as we stood unwavering in the truth. We allowed them to transform and leave once and for all.

A new more expansive space of power emanated.

Many times, we have celebrated all the magic and miracles that happened along the way—from money miracles, the abundant flow of clients, launching back-to-back group coaching programs, collapsing time and getting years of work completed in a very short time, to raising our visibility as we broke through deeper levels of programming that allowed us to expand even more. The whole experience allowed us to float in bliss.

It's now your turn.

You have received infinite love and possibilities from these fourteen stories. There is no more undoing it. You cannot un-see, un-hear, and un-know the truth of what is possible for you. Because you have received the energies of these stories, you are now ripe to fully step into the transformation that your heart has been yearning for. Your True Power is now primed to unleash itself within you!

You have access to *Your True Power* now. It can be as simple as acknowledging and accepting this truth. And if you want additional support in unlocking it, feel free to reach out to the co-authors. Their contact information is at the back of the book, and they will most lovingly assist you.

You're at the end of the book, but this is not the end of the story. It is just the beginning. To help you get started, we curated the top tools that helped 

each co-author to overcome their biggest challenge. download it at www.yourtruepowerbook. com or https://bit.ly/yourtruepowerbook

Keep in touch! Let's connect through email and on social media. Visit our bios in the next section for contact details.

If you need help, please email hello@trissatis.com

Can't wait to hear your *Your True Power* story and share it with the world in the next anthology!

Trissa Tismal-Capili

Enjoyed *Your True Power?*
Please leave a review of the book at your
favorite online retailer (or all of them!).
Thank you!

Acknowledgment

No amount of words can encapsulate our depth of gratitude for everything and everyone that made this book possible.

First and foremost, our deepest gratitude to you, the reader. Thank you so much for receiving our labor of love. We appreciate your time, investment, and openness in reading each of the stories. Dear reader, this has all been for you. Thank you for inspiring us every step of the way.

Overflowing gratitude to our family and friends who have been there every step of the way, supporting us through the writing, publishing, and promoting of this book. Thank you so much for passionately spreading the word about *Your True Power* with us. We so infinitely appreciate and recognize that you went out of your way because you loved us and believed in us wholeheartedly. None of this would have been possible without you. Thank you so much!

To Marci Shimoff, Michael Bernard Beckwith, Dr. Bradley Nelson, Mary Morrissey, Mark Anthony Lord, Petrea King, Steve Olsher, and Rikka Zimmerman, our spiritual mentors, guides, friends, and colleagues. Our deep immense gratitude for your part in our growth and expansion. Utmost thanks and appreciation for your words of support and endorsement of *Your True Power*!

To Rikka Zimmerman, our beloved teacher and friend. Infinite abounding gratitude to you for introducing us to each other in your coaching program and for being so authentic and fully embodying oneness. Your love has deeply empowered us to shine. We get to live in love because you chose to show up in your magnificence. Everlasting thanks to you!

To our publisher, Leaders Press; print and bookstore distribution partner, Simon & Schuster; our foreign rights agent and library distribution team; our editors, copywriters, and graphic designers; RHG Media and audiobook team; promotional partners, influencers, and podcasts that spread the word; our administrative team and Infology, our tech support team—many oceans of thanks to all of you for your tireless support in making all this possible.

Debbie Shuman Espinoza, thank you for your bionic eyes and for spotting the typos in the final proof. You're an angel!

To every person and circumstance that brought us to our knees in deep despair, thank you for giving us the context from which to rise and experience the glorious contrast of being in true power.

To God and the Archangel of *Your True Power*, eternal gratitude for your guidance and support every step of the way. Thank you so much for clearly showing and entrusting us with your vision. Thank you for giving us the gift of being the vehicles for your book.

To my co-authors—Suyen, Leslie, Debbie, Heather, Fiorella, Dawn, Sandra, Aurora, Judith, Barbara, Silvia,

Dionnie, and Gale—endless gratitude for your choice to end separation, share your stories with the world, and stand in *Your True Power*. It is a privilege to witness you shine even brighter. Humanity is now forever changed because of you. On behalf of God and the angels, thank you, thank you, thank you!

I wish it was possible to mention everyone, but to anyone and everyone else who touched us and made this possible, you know who you are. Infinite gratitude to you!

Finally, I would like to express my love and gratitude to my mom, Editha; my late dad, Danni; without whom this book would not have come into existence; my husband, Andrew; my kids, Aden, Andre, Allyson, and Niko; and to the greatest teacher of all: life.

About the Authors

Trissa Tismal-Capili, also known as TrissaTC helps established impact-driven entrepreneurs reach the masses, multiply their impact and skyrocket their business in absolute ease. She is passionate about helping them master the state of flow to grow their business without hurting their personal life, mental health and well-being.

She is a USA Today and Wall Street Journal Bestselling Author, a certified professional coach and speaker with over 20 years of experience, helping thousands of entrepreneurs from start-ups, to coaching multimillion dollar business owners and advising billionaires.

After graduating Magna Cum Laude in Psychology, Trissa co-founded a nationally successful continuing legal education company in the Philippines, and later pursued her passion in personal development in the US. Her obsession with learning and growth gained her a multitude of tools, accreditations and designations, including Certified Professional Coactive Coach, Certified Money, Marketing and Soul Coach, and Certified Advanced Life Transformed Coach, among others. Trissa is always learning and innovating, and continues to receive high level mentorship from the top experts in the fields of success, money, marketing, mindset, spirituality, and publishing.

Trissa has been featured in major media including CBS News, NBC and Fox. She loves guesting on leading-edge podcasts and speaking on renowned stages, including the prestigious Columbia University. She also loves interviewing world leaders in consciousness, business and success, including top New York Times Bestselling Authors.

Trissa is on a big mission to revolutionize the business world by promoting the holistic integration of practical strategies with mind, body and spirit as a norm in business development, and to bring conscious entrepreneurs in front of the masses as the top trusted resource. Through her efforts, she aims to inspire a global shift towards a more abundant heart-centered business model that nurtures a healthy workplace and a thriving customer experience, ultimately leading to a more awakened and sustainable planet.

Email: hello@trissatis.com
Phone: +1 (818) 237-3494
Website: www.trissatis.com
Facebook: @trissatis
LinkedIn: @trissatis
Twitter: @trissatis
Instagram: @trissatis

Leslie Sandra Black has been fascinated since childhood with the mystical dimension of reality. Divine Presence and Love is as alive to her as the three-dimensional world of ordinary experience and separation. Her own inspired journey exploring diverse spiritual paths offers guidance for those on their own quest.

For over forty years, Leslie has transmitted embodied, heart-centered energy healing to facilitate people to find their freedom and their own gifts. Like a lighthouse, Leslie delights in guiding people home into their hearts to be the light and love that they truly are. Colleagues and clients describe Leslie as a "Master Guide" and a "Way-Show-er". She brings a holistic transformative approach to how we relate to our bodies. Leslie enthusiastically models and teaches how to access our own body wisdom as profound guidance for our lives.

Leslie draws upon her extensive training in diverse healing and coaching modalities as a teacher and speaker—as well as with groups, individuals, and through facilitation over distance.

She is especially drawn to support other healers and helping professionals, who, like herself, have been taught to serve by bearing the pain and distress of others and the world.

She holds steady a vision that the purpose for humanity is to awaken into fully embodying the divine essence we truly are. As humanity awakens, the world will evolve and transform! Leslie's writing, teaching, and personal facilitation embody that vision.

Email: leslie@heartawakening.ca
Website: www.heartawakening.ca
Facebook Pages:
- Heart Awakening Transformational Coaching & Energy Healing
- Leslie Sandra Black

Certified in several healing modalities, **Suyen Bailey**'s approach to life coaching and energy healing facilitation is very unique and customized. She believes that everyone is in a different level of consciousness and awareness with incomparable backgrounds and experiences. She is gentle, warm, compassionate, and firm; and her sessions, workshops, and seminars are healing, interactive, fun, and educational.

Suyen was born and raised by traditional Roman Catholic parents in the Philippines. She attended an all-girls Catholic private school from kindergarten to college where she earned her bachelor's in business administration. In 1982, she took fashion design in California to pursue her dream of becoming a fashion designer. With high hopes and ambition, she moved to the Fashion Capital of the World, New York City, where she also attended a Charm/Finishing School. It is in the "Big Apple" where she met her ex-husband. The trajectory of her dream went from working as an assistant fashion designer on Seventh Avenue to an abused wife and mother of three for twenty-three years.

Being in an abusive relationship, Suyen's journey from darkness to light became an unending quest of self-discovery, self-realization and self-empowerment. Instead of therapy, she chose to study one healing modality after another until the present. She did not only evolve to be an empowered woman, but also healed herself from chronic fatigue, allergies, depression, physical pain, etc. Initially, just to heal herself, she uses her life challenges, fourteen years knowledge of energy healing and coaching as opportunities to help others.

Suyen is a Life Transformed certified coach in life and business coaching, hypnosis, Reiki (levels 1-2), Emotion Code, Spontaneous Transformation Technique (levels 1-2), Life Transformed Advanced Coaching, Ho-oponopono, Genesis Point Healing level 1 and knowledge of other techniques that she mixes and matches.

Website: authenticheartsignature.net

Born to Hungarian immigrant parents in New Jersey, **Judith Krug** has bravely journeyed her path to enlightenment to become the woman she is now. Starting with Erhard Seminars Training (EST), Relationship, Miracle of Love, and continuing with Rikka Zimmerman's Life Transformed program, Judith took control of her life and built a strong foundation to understand the deeper meaning of existence.

She is now a certified Advanced Life Coach and has learned how to create an abundant life full of gratitude and joy. She resides in Los Angeles, California, where she runs a successful mortgage brokerage business. She helps buyers and homeowners set up non-conforming equity-based loans funded by private investors, originating over 30 million dollars in loans a year.

Judith is dedicated to serving others with her wealth of knowledge by supporting them through their journey to enlightenment, abundance, and gratitude.

Website: www.judithkrug.com

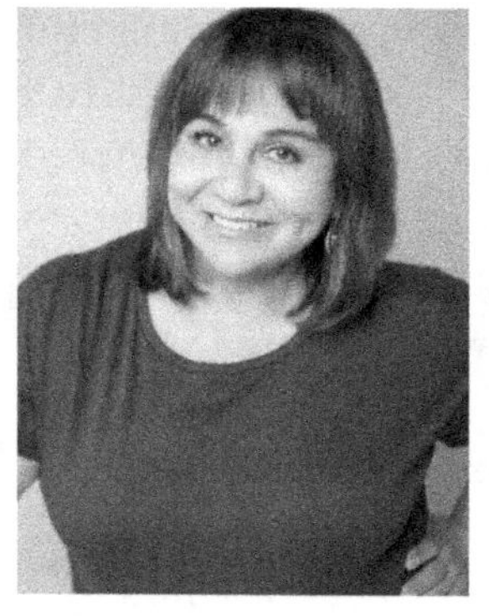

Silvia Rios is a certified Advanced Life Transformed Coach, registered physical therapist, spiritual counselor, and meditation teacher. She lives in Chicago and Florida and is dedicated to facilitating people in finding their inner light to experience the magic of living.

In her free time, she enjoys traveling and connecting with people from all over the world. Her desire for communication inspired her to learn different languages, and she speaks English, Spanish, Italian, and is pursuing French. Her experience in the medical field working as a scrub nurse for many years and as a home care physical therapist allows her to guide her coaching clients in understanding the correlation between the emotional, energetic, and physical planes as the originators of disease in the body so they can consciously choose health and well-being. She also assists people in releasing self-judgment to embody the beauty of being.

She brings knowledge from various disciplines she has studied over the years, such as Lifeline technique, neurolinguistic programming, Feldenkrais Method, Access Consciousness, and Shiatzu.

Her mission is to bring awareness so people can step into the Creator position in their lives to experience Love, Joy, and Peace.

Silvia is available for coaching and classes in person or online internationally.

Website: www.silviarios.com
Facebook: Silvia Rios Coaching
LinkedIn: Silvia Rios

Fiorella Garibaldi is an embodied energy coach, yoga teacher, breathworker, and international retreat facilitator. She helps people connect back into their bodies, their hearts, and their truth through ancient wisdom, intuitive energy work, and embodiment practices.

Her passion is for everyone to experience themselves as the true source of everything they need, empowering them to look within for answers and experience their full potential in every single moment.

She was born in Peru, lived in the USA for most of her life, until recently moving to Sweden. She holds a very strong bond with her Peruvian roots, bringing her shamanic connection, her love for nature, and her connection to the elements to all her practices. Her love for inner exploration and adventures has led her to travel the world, expanding her experience and obtaining certifications as a yoga teacher in Bali and Miami, a life transformed coach in Hawaii, a breathwork certification in Miami, a theta healing practitioner in Los Angeles and currently immersing herself in activating the voice as a mean of vibrational healing in Colombia.

Website : www.fiorellagaribaldi.com

Sandra Ann Grant is a Life Transformed™ Advanced Certified Coach. Sandy is a mother, dancer, poet, writer, artist, facilitator; intuitive, curious, inquisitive, ever-learning.

From a corporate background in finance and systems, she draws on over twenty-eight years' experience as teacher, trainer, coach, mentor, water polo at international level, professional dance, and her own personal hardships to empower you to live a life of "infinite possibilities."

Her own transformation was from "not good enough", abuse, low self-esteem, losing love/family, home, health, money to living in a state of abundance, joy, trust, and self-love.

Based in Sydney, Australia she coaches by telephone or online.

Email: sandy@sandyempowers.com
Website: www.SandyEmpowers.com
Facebook: Sandy Empowers; Connect Through Sandy
LinkedIn: sandygrant-sydney

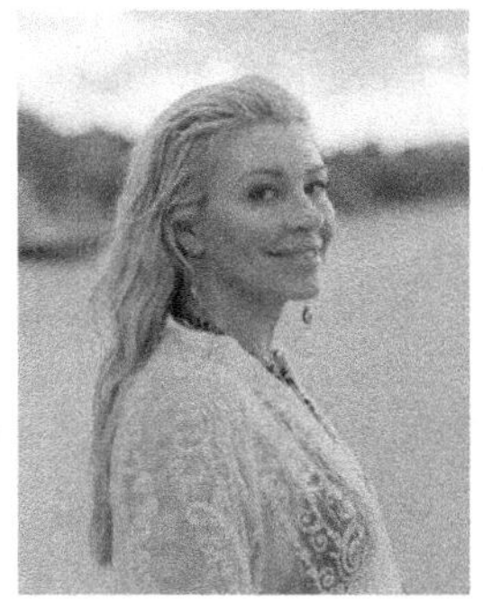**Dionnie Simone** is a yoga instructor and a loving, kind, and compassionate meditation teacher and consciousness facilitator. Dionnie enjoys writing poetry, blogs, and staying fit and healthy. Much of her time is spent designing courses and adding and editing empowering content for her yoga and meditation YouTube channel. She has completed thousands of hours with mentors, completing a transcendental meditation course, meditations, Medihealings, and live events with Mas Sajady throughout the U. S becoming a Healing Mastery Advanced Alumni.

Dionnie is a qualified (two hundred hours) yoga instructor and Life Transformed coach (under the tutelage of Rikka Zimmerman). She lives and breathes her craft, taking herself and others beyond perceived limitations.

Personal writing has been a focus the past seven years and has been very cathartic. Painting is another of her creative outlets. She encourages people to imagine, choose consciously, and move away from fear into love. Her message is all about regaining your power and steering yourself back into creative control of your own life. It's been a while since her first publication. In fifth grade, a magazine article by a well-known Australian writer and broadcaster Phillip Adams featured her story about meeting Phillip Adams and travelling to school in an apple! She lives with her partner, Sash, and three fur babies in Melbourne, Australia. Find out more at www.astrayoga.com.au.

Email: astrayoga.life@gmail.com
Facebook: @astrayoga.life
Twitter: @DionnieSimone
YouTube: Dionnie Simone - Yoga & Meditation
Instagram: @astrayoga.life

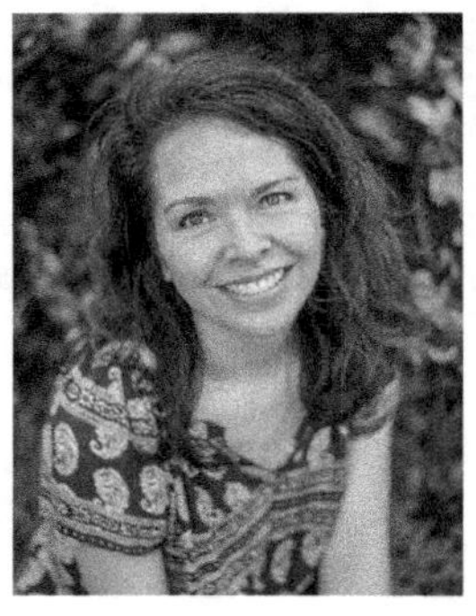

Barbara Harumi Otis is a life-long learner, energy facilitator, and life coach who assists others to create positive shifts in their lives by using an eclectic mix of various healing modalities.

Barbara has been a lifelong seeker. After overcoming a painful divorce through deep soul healing, she finally realized that what she was searching for was inside her. She learned that she could never find the happiness she was searching for outside herself.

It is now her mission to assist spiritual seeking women reconnect to their own wisdom, power, and joy, so they can create a life they love. She helps people who are always looking for more but can't seem to find what they are looking for no matter how hard they try. She helps them create, design, and live the life of their dreams. She holds space for them to heal, release, or integrate what has been getting in the way.

Barbara's most current certifications include: Life Transformed Advanced Certified Coach, Sacred Soul Alignment Practitioner, Energetic Allergy Healing Advanced Practitioner, and Sacred Light Advanced Practitioner. She has studied self-help and energy work for over thirty years and also has certifications in Reconnective Healing (levels 1–3), Quantum Touch (QT Practitioner, Supercharging, and Core Transformation), Brain Gym (Teacher Practicum), ARCH (Kaula Practitioner), I'O (Infinite Oneness Master), Symmetry (levels 1&2), and Reiki (levels 1–3).

She homeschooled her two now-adult boys. Barbara loves to travel, dance, and spend time in nature.

Website: www.BarbaraHarumi.com

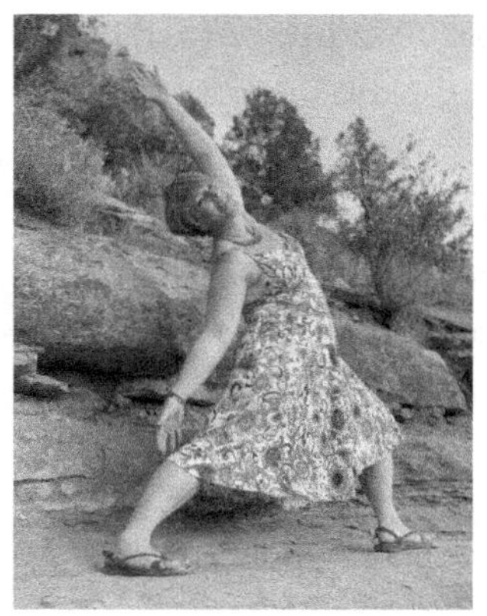

Dawn Gomez is most inspired by nature and its infinite abundance of gifts that reflect our life. She loves choosing to wander in wonder in her hometown woods of northwestern New Jersey and around the globe. Nature constantly reminds her of the ever-present truth of love with gifts of hearts in rocks, trees, clouds, flowers, food, and even as a new freckle on her wrist.

Dawn created and opened Garden of Life Massage & Yoga Center in 2003 where she expresses her heart through her bodywork as a licensed massage therapist in New Jersey and New York, specializing in Tuina, Chinese medical massage, and manual lymphatic drainage, as a registered yoga teacher, Qigong, and laughter yoga teacher, and as a Life Transformed coach. She was drawn to these practices through her own healing journey from migraines, chronic pain, overwhelm, and not feeling good enough. Garden of Life has received multiple accolades from the Sussex County Chamber of Commerce and NJAWBO (New Jersey Association of Women Business Owners), and as the *New Jersey Herald*'s Readers' Choice as Sussex County's Best Massage.

To assist her clients explore their own incredible talents and gifts, Dawn provides single day and multi-day retreats in beautiful destinations sharing her love of nature, travel, and play.

Email: dawn@dawngomez.com
Phone: +1 (973) 903 7508
Website: www.dawngomez.com
Facebook: @l.dawn.gomez; @GardenofLifeMassage
Instagram: @dlightofday

 **Heather Ann Fink** is a certified life transformation coach who specializes in mentoring people who love deeply but struggle with repeating painful patterns in their intimate relationships, to experience the *joyful and nourishing intimacy and connections* they desire.

She is deeply fulfilled by expertly teaching clients a path to freedom beyond learned patterns and coping strategies that were initiated in traumatic experiences, so they can confidently step into a life that is *self-authored, pleasurable and deeply satisfying.*

Heather's own life models the transformation that is possible for her clients, through standing in the fire, identifying unhealthy behaviors in herself and her relationships, and her commitment to the deep work of shifting her own beliefs, conditioning and limitations as they have arisen. She has created a new life for herself that she loves and has been able to step powerfully into the freedom she always hoped was possible!

From almost two decades of professional development and client care she develops signature programs. The programs provide her clients with a step-by-step path to help transform the distressing and exhausting patterns found in hurtful relationships. She mentors her clients to realize and integrate new ways of relating that are rooted in the understanding that *loving deeply doesn't have to be so hard,* and a new freedom beyond what they've previously imagined is waiting for them.

Website: www.heatherannfink.com

Gale Ziccarelli, MSW, LCSW. Gale has a master's degree in social work and is a licensed clinical social worker. She is certified in EMDR and EFT and trained in relaxation therapy, which is a powerful tool that involves visualization. As a psychotherapist for eighteen years, Gale specialized in treating depression, women's issues, and stress management. She helped thousands of clients improve their mental health and master valuable coping skills. She worked with adults and teens providing both individual and couples therapy.

Gale believes in treating the body as a whole, so she focuses on helping people discover and maintain balance in the areas of mind, body, and spirit. Currently, as a certified Advanced Life Transformed coach, she helps individuals transform their lives by combining her knowledge of mental health with her new life coaching skills. In this way, she provides a unique therapeutic experience whereby she helps people release blocks that hold them back from living their best life.

Her deeper mission is to empower women to become their authentic self so they can have a fulfilling, joyful life. Gale holds a vision of peace, love, and joy for both herself and the planet. She enjoys practicing yoga. She has two sons and one grandson, and she currently lives in Wisconsin.

Website: www.awakeningsbygale.com
Facebook: @awakeningsbyGale

Aurora Hammond lives on the Sunshine Coast in Queensland, Australia. She has been a facilitator of personal growth for over thirty years, having studied in Australia, the United Kingdom, the United States, and parts of Asia. She has been a lecturer in social work at the University of NSW and Tasmania and founded and ran her own college of holistic counselling for nearly twenty years in Sydney, Australia.

In her master's degree in holistic studies (psychology), she learned the value of sharing your own story as part of leading the way for others and having compassion and deep empathy for the human journey. Her focus on her spiritual path as the "true journey of the soul" and the power of working consciously in the quantum field inspire her current practice. Aurora's wisdom and experience combined with her insight and love of quantum consciousness exploration make her webinars, workshops, and one-to-one facilitation a truly unique and enriching experience.

Website: aurorahoodhammond.com
Phone: +61 411 164 732
Email: team@aurorahoodhammond.com
Facebook: @aurorahoodhammond
Instagram: aurorahoodhammond

Transformational Leader **Debbie Shuman Espinoza** is the Worthiness Warrior. She is an award-winning, #1 best-selling author of *Wakening Your Worth*, speaker, life transformation/self-love facilitator, and international entrepreneur.

Winner of the Rising Star Award, she has studied self-help and personal development for over seven years. She holds numerous workshops and classes where she speaks and teaches about claiming the worthiness we were born with and ending the shame we hide.

Debbie has overcome many obstacles in her life, among them the death of her husband when she was just thirty-four, her thirty-year addiction to prescription drugs, and much, much more. This has inspired her to become a writer and speaker who is passionate about helping others change their lives, triumph over hardships, and realize their dreams.

Debbie is a widowed mother of three amazing children, who have always believed in her and supported her. Because of them and their love, she has been able to reclaim her life and finally realize her potential. She now wants others to know they too can also rewrite their story, claim their worth, and live their dreams.

Website: www.theworthinesswarrior.com
Facebook: Debbie Shuman Espinoza
Instagram: TheWorthinessWarrior

HELP SPREAD
YOUR TRUE POWER

AND MAKE THIS WORLD A BETTER PLACE

 Leave a review of the book at your favorite online retailer (or all of them!)

 Share it on social media #yourtruepowerbook

 Gift it to family and friends

 Be The Change!

Notes

Notes

Notes

Notes

Notes

Notes

Notes

Notes

HELP SPREAD
YOUR TRUE POWER

AND MAKE THIS WORLD A BETTER PLACE

- Leave a review of the book at your favorite online retailer (or all of them!)

- Share it on social media #yourtruepowerbook

- Gift it to family and friends

- Be The Change!

YOUR TRUE POWER

THE KEY TO YOUR
Amazing Life

By

Trissa Tismal-Capili

With
Suyen Angbetic Bailey
Leslie Sandra Black
Debbie Shuman Espinoza
Heather Ann Fink
Fiorella Garibaldi
Dawn Gomez
Sandra Ann Grant
Aurora Hood Hammond
Judith Krug
Barbara Harumi Otis
Silvia Rios
Dionnie Simone
Gale Ziccarelli

Copyright © 2021 Trissa Tismal-Capili
Published in the United States by Leaders Press
www.leaderspress.com

ISBN 978-1-63735-313-4 (pbk)
ISBN 978-1-7353943-0-5 (ebook)

Library of Congress Control Number: 2021903680